Humanity and the Enemy

HUMANITY AND THE ENEMY

HOW ETHICS CAN RID POLITICS OF VIOLENCE

Bruno Gullì

HUMANITY AND THE ENEMY

Copyright © Bruno Gullì, 2014.

First published in 2014 by PALGRAVE MACMILLAN® in the United States—a division of St. Martin's Press LLC, 175 Fifth Avenue, New York, NY 10010.

Where this book is distributed in the UK, Europe and the rest of the world, this is by Palgrave Macmillan, a division of Macmillan Publishers Limited, registered in England, company number 785998, of Houndmills, Basingstoke, Hampshire RG21 6XS.

Palgrave Macmillan is the global academic imprint of the above companies and has companies and representatives throughout the world.

Palgrave® and Macmillan® are registered trademarks in the United States, the United Kingdom, Europe and other countries.

ISBN: 978-1-137-45647-2

Library of Congress Cataloging-in-Publication Data is available from the Library of Congress.

A catalogue record of the book is available from the British Library.

Design by Scribe Inc.

First edition: November 2014

10 9 8 7 6 5 4 3 2 1

Transferred to Digital Printing in 2015

Stay human

—Vittorio Arrigoni

For Nino, Angela, and Nino

CONTENTS

ACKNOWLEDGMENTS

The idea for this book started a little over a year ago. I had the opportunity to present it to Brian O'Connor of Palgrave Macmillan at the Left Forum Conference in New York City in 2013. His enthusiastic support was essential in shaping my determination to write it. So I thank him a lot for that. When I was in Italy this past winter, I read some sections I had written to my sister, Angela, and my friends, Nino Quaranta and Antonio Tramontana. Their comments and questions were invaluable. Nino, who is a member of SOS Rosarno, greatly helped me to get an understanding of the situation of the African migrants in the Rosarno area and in Calabria. He introduced me to Ibrahim Diabate and Lamine Bodian, who are from the Ivory Coast and Senegal, respectively, and are also members of SOS Rosarno. The conversations I had with them were also extremely helpful. At the end of January, I traveled to Lampedusa, where I met members of the Askavusa Collective. That was an extraordinary experience, which I look forward to repeating. Back in New York, the classes I taught at Kingsborough Community College, as well as the class I am coteaching with Peter Bratsis and the participation of Michael Pelias among others at the Brecht Forum, gave me a further opportunity to think through some of the concepts and problems I present and deal with in the book. I then thank the students and participants in both situations. The remark on Machiavelli is based on a paper I delivered at the Left Forum Conference of 2013. Parts of Chapter 5 are based on a paper I published in

Im@go: Rivista di Studi Sociali sull'Immaginario and on a paper I delivered at the Left Forum Conference of 2012. For the latter, I received input and critical comments from Shana Siegel, Linden Lewis, and Hilbourne Watson, who were on the panel with me. Finally, I thank my twin brother, Nino, who read the whole manuscript and gave me invaluable help and advice.

Introduction

The title of this book, *Humanity and the Enemy*, intends to call into question one of Carl Schmitt's most striking statements in *The Concept of the Political*. The statement in question is, "Humanity is not a political concept" (Schmitt 1996: 55). This statement is very central in Schmitt's theory and has a twofold function: on the one hand, it is the result (and thus perhaps the proof) of his notion of politics as the relationship of friend and enemy, while being its very presupposition on the other hand. Indeed, the friend-and-enemy logic makes sense only insofar as humanity is excluded from the realm of politics, and this exclusion is both a presupposition and a result of the type of politics Schmitt has in mind. However, precisely, what kind of politics can it be that excludes humanity? Who are the actors in it, and what are its aims? A brief answer is that this is a politics that, in excluding humanity, also excludes ethics. Humanity would indeed be an ethical, rather than political, concept. However, this so-called autonomy of the political raises very serious issues. Notably, what will be the use of politics if politics is understood as being completely independent of ethics and any moral consideration? We know that for Aristotle, for instance, ethics is part of the political sciences. Both politics (the science of the community) and ethics (the science of freedom) are required for the construction of the good life, happiness, and a world of justice. It, then, seems that excluding humanity from the realm of the political turns politics into a mere game. No longer an instrument for the actualization of the good life, it becomes a skirmish between friend and enemy, winner and loser; it becomes a basic structure of total and permanent war—a war without which, it seems, there is no hope for security. In a rather consistent fashion, Schmitt denies that the political can have any claim to universality—which is what a long and rich tradition of thinking would certainly attribute to the ethical. Thus the particularistic logic of the friend-and-enemy relationship becomes the essential trait of the political and what distinguishes it from the ethical or any other domain (e.g., the economy, culture, and so on).

What I want to argue in this book is that the concept of the political so narrowly defined, the autonomy of the political from ethics and other domains and the exclusion of humanity from its scope, is not what the political needs to be. Indeed, this is simply the concept of the status quo in politics and of so-called political "realism." However, it makes sense to think of the unity of politics and ethics as an alternative to a world that seems unable or unwilling to deliver conditions of social justice and the good life for all—where "for all" means a humanity that has surpassed the friend-and-enemy impasse, having perhaps eliminated the very concept or possibility of the enemy. An emblematic example of this alternative is offered by Vittorio Arrigoni's simple yet provocative imperative, "Stay human," which I use as an epigraph for this book. Arrigoni's imperative as well as his devotion to the cause of the Palestinians in Gaza and his untimely and tragic death are a clear sign of the problematic nature of thinking and practicing the unity of the ethical and the political. They are obviously also a sign of the danger of this unity and thus of its ability to upset forms of politics and thinking that should by now have become obsolete.[1] Another way to put this is to say, with Vilho Harle, that it is not "the *Enemy* but the Enemy *thought*" that must be overcome (Harle 2000: 190). Obviously, this cannot simply be the result of a thinking exercise. For this to happen, it is necessary to create new material conditions for an effective and universal access to the good life; new relations of power grounded in care rather than domination; and just as was the case with Arrigoni's exemplary activism, a new culture that opposes war and violence as well as the notions of difference and the other as negative and problematic notions. What seems certain is that the friend-and-enemy logic—whether in the precise, technical sense formulated by Schmitt or in the generalized sense whereby the enemy is also seen as the evil one—does not allow for anything else but the reproduction of a culture and reality of permanent war. It is also true that even Schmitt's technical notion of the enemy cannot avoid becoming a category in a moralistic and pseudoethical way of thinking grounded in the simplistic and pernicious logic of good and evil, where "we" are of course always "good" and "they" are "evil." This is the type of thinking that has prevailed, for instance, in the current so-called war on terror—a type of thinking that is creating the conditions for the destruction of humanity itself.

Interestingly, although Schmitt was a conservative thinker, his definition of the political as the relationship of friend and enemy and his notion of the autonomy of the political sphere have become important for progressive (antiliberal) thinkers as well. There are important reasons for this. The distance of the political from the ethical is fundamental, especially for people working from within the Marxist tradition who welcome Schmitt's theory. There is thus an agreement that humanity is not a political concept, and this is generally reflected in the suspicion of the doctrine of human rights, international law, and all talk of humanitarianism. While this is all very important, it also makes sense to consider the possibility of an alternative to what seems to be an either-or situation. It is of course true that Marx also spoke against focusing on the issue of rights insofar as that is a path to bourgeois individualism. However, this does not exhaust the potentiality of the concept of humanity; for that matter, Marx did not dismiss that concept, but on the contrary he upheld it, as human emancipation was at the center of his revolutionary theory and science of history.

We are often told that relying on the concept of humanity and the notion of human rights is inconsistent with Marxist thinking, especially because Marx saw these rights as bourgeois privilege rights and because this way of thinking may eliminate the centrality of the class struggle. However, I do not believe that this is the case. In truth, a revolutionary, radical concept of humanity emerges precisely from firmly holding on to the reality of the class struggle and universalizing human rights is another name for a world in which there is social justice. It seems to me that any thinking that concerns itself with true social justice—that is, a world in which the material principles of justice are such that literally everyone does have access to a decent or good life—cannot avoid dealing with what today goes under the name of human rights, and that includes Marxism. To be sure, the question has been investigated. For instance, in an informative article published in *Rethinking Marxism* some time ago, a group of scholars came to the conclusion that the difference between the human rights approach and the philosophy of Marx is the difference between political and human emancipation (see Gordon, Swanson, and Buttigieg 2000). The focus of the present book is not on the question of human rights but rather on the concept of humanity and thus on the relationship between politics and ethics. However, it seems clear to me that this is precisely what human emancipation entails and presupposes: a type of politics "grounded" in ethics. Yet not one arguing for liberal and individualistic rights but rather one recognizing the universal and common necessity, the fragility, of the human condition. Fragility and necessity become the material for the systems of oppression and exploitation we have known throughout history, including and most notably the present system, the system of capital. The flourishing of the human condition requires the deactivation and abandonment of the system of capital. The latter, with its claim to sovereignty and its implementation of innumerable forms of domination, disfigures and crushes human dignity; it makes human emancipation impossible. If there is any use we can make of Schmitt's intriguing yet problematic thought (but perhaps precisely against its intention), it is to identify the figure of the enemy in the tendential movement of its passing and overcoming. The enemy of humanity is capital—that is, the system of violence that includes the friend-and-enemy relationship, war as a permanent possibility or an actual reality, and the production of miserable conditions of life for a growing number of human beings, as well as the destruction of other forms of life and the earth. However, contrary to what Schmitt indicates, this is not an instance in the general and unsurpassable logic of friend and enemy. It is rather the way in which humanity becomes, precisely, a political concept, not in the sense of defense and security (the friend-and-enemy relationship again), but rather in the sense of flourishing, creating the material and ethical conditions for the good life for literally everyone. This is after all not completely different from the spirit of the philosophy of human rights, despite the fact that its applicability is today thwarted by an old paradigm of the political as well as the lack of true ethical reform. Thus to speak of humanity as a political, as well as ethical, concept does not imply—as Schmitt fears—the paradoxical figure of a war that ends all wars, but rather the overcoming of the dogma that there can be no end to the regime of permanent war.

In his ethical writings, Immanuel Kant distinguishes between practical and pathological love. The latter is an inclination that "cannot be commanded" (1981: 12).

On the contrary, the former "resides in the will and not in the propensities of feeling, in principles of action and not in tender sympathy; and only this practical love can be commanded" (ibid.). This is important as an introduction to his two main ethical principles: the categorical imperative and the kingdom of ends.[2] Kant himself makes a reference to "those passages of Scripture which command us to love our neighbors and even our enemy" (ibid.). Evidently, the latter situation is impossible from the point of view of what he calls "pathological love." Thus he highlights the ethical importance of practical love, which is universal and concrete. However, when the enemy is loved, he or she ceases to be an enemy. The enemy is a political concept, but Kant is speaking in ethical terms. Is this merely an exaggeration? Is it perhaps the case that the political passions and interests that produce the enemy are offset by the ethical command? Are ethics and politics two completely different spheres of life and can we behave differently in each? Probably, the answer to these questions is negative. It is perhaps through an understanding of the categorical imperative and, especially, the kingdom of ends that we can make sense of the practicality of this universal and concrete love. We can perhaps find a place where ethics and politics (a politics other than the one producing the enemy) are interdependent and necessary to one another.

In the preface to *Transcritique*, Kojin Karatani, after denying the view that Kant was a "bourgeois philosopher," says, "In the context of a capitalist economy where people treat each other merely as a means to an end, the Kantian 'kingdom of freedom' or 'kingdom of ends' clearly comes to entail another meaning, that is, communism" (2005: viii). He also says that for Marx, at least the young Marx, "communism was a Kantian categorical imperative, that is, practical and moral par excellence" (xii). He then goes on to establish this relation between Kant and Marx—a relation that is important because it favors the idea of an ethically founded revolutionary politics. In my view, that is the only politics that may meaningfully lay claim to the practicality of social change—a change for a better world not only without exploitation and oppression but also without the constancy of the friend-and-enemy relation. Kant's categorical imperative is useful in this respect because what defines it is its autonomy from any special and particularistic interests and its universal aspiration and scope. Its ideality must be part of a new social and political reality, and it actually must be its foundation and internal structure. It is what alone leads to the idea of freedom properly understood—that is to say, not the freedom to do as one pleases, but rather the freedom to do (or not do) what is right and just according to universal principles. As Karatani says, "Kant thought that freedom lay in the duty to obey (or command) . . . But it is clear that Kant did not identify duty with that which is imposed by the community's code [e.g., the human-made law]. If the command of duty is of community, to obey is a heteronomous act, and not free. In order to be free, then, what kind of command does one have to obey? That is no other than the command: 'be free!'" (118; brackets added). Karatani also points out that this command comes "neither from community nor from God" (ibid.). Indeed, it is the transcendental moral law itself.

The radicality of this conception should be very clear to anyone. God or community (i.e., not only divine or positive law but also the social, moral, and cultural norms that vary from place to place and time to time) cannot be the source of ethics and freedom. A world of social justice cannot be built when people follow the dictates of a religion or of a moral, legal, and cultural code. Instead, social justice resides for Kant in the universality of ethics and the practicality of freedom and in practical love—that is to say, in an ethically founded and driven type of politics.

When politics has no ethical foundation but is cotermi-
nous with the law, the law as command (which is the case
in the world today and ever since Hobbes's formulation
of the theory of sovereignty), there is very little freedom.
We are granted a degree of freedom and various forms of
freedom understood in legal and narrowly political terms.
These freedoms (or rights) can be taken away at any time.
As a matter of fact, our bodies do not belong to us: it is as
if we had leased them, and they are subject to be returned
at any time.

This is the concept of politics I want to contrast with
the previous one. Thus we have two types of politics. One
type of politics is informed by ethics. This can be initially
understood in terms of Kantian philosophy (the categorical imperative and the kingdom of ends), but it then
extends to all forms of revolutionary politics, all forms of
action for social change and social justice. The other type
of politics is completely oblivious to ethics and is determined solely by a positive sense of the law, where the law
is of course nothing but institutionalized might and violence. This is the model we classically find in Hobbes and
later in the decisionist philosophy of Schmitt and all reactionary thought. The concept of the enemy belongs in
both types of politics: in the former as a concept to be
overcome and in the latter as a permanent and necessary
structure. Indeed, for the latter, there is no end in view
to the friend-and-enemy relationship—namely, no end
in view to fear, coercion, and war. For the former, there
is the possibility of a universalizing moment or process
whereby fear and coercion can be overcome, and war—
even in its potentiality—is eliminated. This would be a
world of social justice in which life is no longer organized
and regulated according to the logic of oppression and
domination and violence and exploitation. Let us call the
first type of politics "revolutionary" and the second "reactionary." Reactionary politics remains caught in a vision of

terror, and consequently, a regime of terror. In reactionary politics, the enemy is an agent of terror, which must be fought by building a terror-inspiring offensive (think of the current drone war, for instance). Revolutionary politics recognizes that there is an enemy (e.g., the system) and that it is necessary to deactivate and dismantle the conditions for the possibility of its reproduction. It also recognizes that the worst enemy is, precisely, the enemy thought. However, revolutionary politics envisions a time in which there no longer is an enemy or the enemy thought, and thus it avoids the trap and danger of permanent war and terror. In fact, permanent war is what reactionary politics needs in order to sustain itself and reproduce its particularistic and inhuman interests. It is true that the overcoming of the regime of war is what Hobbes wanted. However, for Hobbes, the price to be paid for that was the loss of all freedom under a coercive regime of punishment and fear. Essentially, one gives up the original fear present in the state of nature for the new kind of fear determined by the oppressive power of the state. For Hobbes, the passage from the state of nature (the war of everybody against everybody) to the state of political society is not one in which the potentiality of the former completely disappears in the actuality of the latter. In fact, a relapse into the state of nature remains always possible, so it is a psychological, not a historical and dialectical, passage. However, even in that sense, it is evident that Hobbes's requirements do not allow humanity to exit the regime of war and enter a situation of security and peace. This is so not simply because the state of nature always, as it were, lurks behind, but rather because that is what the political state and the law as command can deliver. This is probably due to the fact that coercion in general and the coercive laws in particular are not at all the ways to bring about that change—namely, the passage from permanent war to true peace. Instead, what must change is twofold: (1) the material conditions of life and (2) the ethical disposition of humanity. Only a type of politics working toward these ends can be called revolutionary. The first end is accomplished through a radically new form of production, one that is not obsessed with security and growth but rather interested in care, sustainable development, and degrowth. The second end is accomplished through a radically new form of education, which has self-education (or the care of the self) at its center and, to use Antonio Gramsci's words, "intellectual and moral reform" as a pointer (1971: 133).

The present book is not arguing for replacing politics with ethics but rather for the urgency of rethinking politics *on the basis* and *from the viewpoint of* ethics. Perhaps, one way of putting this would be to say that the relationship of politics to ethics is that of means to end. However, this might be a somewhat simplified account of a relationship that is more complex than that. It is difficult to argue that politics is an end in itself, but it makes sense to say that an ethically just world is the end of politics. The main point, however, is that politics and ethics cannot (should not) be separated. Any form of politics devoid of ethics leads to one form or another of abuse, corruption, violence, and lack of transparency. At the same time, when all emphasis is on ethics and politics is forgone, one has an idealistic system of justice, which might have no bearing on the real world. It is important then not to lose sight of the necessary union of politics and ethics; or, to put it differently, the synthesis of necessity and possibility. The aim is to explore ways of setting a new course to human history, the human adventure. This book intends to be a reflection on this theme.

In Chapter 1, "Ethics and the Law: Reconsidering the Friend-and-Enemy Logic," I discuss the notions of fear and the enemy. The emphasis is on the thought of Hobbes, Schmitt, and Kant. I start with a close reading of some of the central passages from Hobbes's *Leviathan*, where he formulates his theory of sovereignty and of the law as command. I, then, discuss some of the most important concepts in Schmitt's theory of political decisionism, and I end with Kant's ethical critique of what he calls the pathological law and his main ethical concepts: the categorical imperative and the kingdom of ends. The point is to stress the meaning of dignity in order to counter the idea of the autonomy of the political and search for an alternative to it.

This chapter has a section discussing Machiavelli and the desire for freedom. In this section, I try to challenge the common view that Machiavelli has no concern at all for ethics, and I argue that his political ontology of the potential (which is part of his understanding of the real) is also immediately ethical—though of course not moralistic—in character. I do so by also looking at Gramsci's reading of Machiavelli in *The Prison Notebooks*.

In Chapter 2, "The Ethical Obligation to Disobey and Resist," I focus on Martin Luther King's "Letter from a Birmingham Jail" and on Sophocles's *Antigone*. What emerges from the reading of both works is the notion that acts of disobedience and resistance are not simply *right*: we actually have an ethical duty to engage in them. Resistance to the unjust law and noncompliance with an unjust order, which are seen by the pathological law as contemptuous and criminal, are in truth ways in which human dignity is saved and restored. If anything, it is the pathological law itself that shows contempt for humanity and life when it criminalizes resistance and dissent. In discussing these issues, I give some examples from recent situations of resistance and struggle, such as the Arab Spring and Occupy Wall Street. One important point, which I then take up again in Chapters 4 and 5, is the issue of resistance, violence, and counterviolence.

Chapter 3, "Deactivate Violence: Human Insecurity, the Enemy, and the Other," is a discussion of the current global obsession with issues of security, which results in great insecurity for many people, especially the weakest and neediest. The main notion to be considered is the one encapsulated in the typical excuse used after a police or military use of excessive force: *We apologize; it was unfortunate. But of course it was done for 'your' protection.* The chapter starts with the Miami airport incident some years ago in which a man suffering from bipolar disorder was shot dead by airport police when he appeared as a threat to them, and it will emphasize the issue of disability in this context. Centered on the issue of police and military brutality (in particular in cities such as New York and in the world), it also includes a discussion of the current drone war. Here we see that the enemy is anyone who fits the description of the other from the viewpoint of a logic and politics of identity in which a self, which does not see itself as another, assumes its superiority and exceptionality.

In Chapter 4, "Labor, Poverty, and Migration: Sovereign Terror and the War against Humanity," I consider some aspects of the philosophy of Marx, especially around the issues of rights and humanity, poverty and wealth, and labor and capital. The chapter deals with the difference between political and human emancipation, focusing on issues of class, race, and migration. For instance, a reference is made to the African migrants arriving in Lampedusa, Italy, on their way to other places in Europe or drowning in the Mediterranean before they reach Lampedusa. This chapter goes back to the issue of resistance discussed in Chapter 2, especially with reference to the initial stage of the Arab Spring. From the viewpoint of established, institutional power, the other is always potentially an enemy, which must be dealt with according to a politics of war, of shock and awe, control and punishment. However, what must be eliminated from politics is not the concept of humanity, which for Schmitt simply does not belong in it, but that of war. The chapter ends with two significant illustrations of political and cultural projects that promote an exit from the logic of the enemy and the construction of an alternative. The projects I consider are those of SOS Rosarno in Calabria and the Askavusa Collective in Lampedusa.

Chapter 5, "Deactivating Terror and the Enemy Logic," initially intended to be a discussion of the notion "aiding the enemy," focusing on the stories of Chelsea (Bradley) Manning and Edward Snowden. The idea was that of stressing that often aiding the enemy is only a misnomer for doing what the ethical obligation requires. I have treated this question in Chapter 2, especially with reference to *Antigone*, and I have referred to it in Chapter 1 when I speak of Schmitt. In the current chapter, I then focus on the biopolitical implications of this war against humanity and ethical principles, and I also deal with aspects of the critique of violence, necessary for a reappropriation of the theoretical instruments to be used in the process of deactivating the global network of terror. However, the current institutional politics of fear and terror construes as criminal (or potentially criminal) any action dictated by ethics, which aims at the universal plane of humanity and dignity. It is then very important to stress that counterviolence and resistance are not ways of perpetuating the logic of the enemy and of war, but rather processes by which this logic might ultimately be overcome. In this chapter, I review some important concepts by Michel Foucault, and I also deal with Frantz Fanon's analysis of the question of violence and counterviolence.

The conclusion points out once again the importance of fighting for the overcoming of the logic of violence, war, and the enemy and the importance of resistance. It also claims that there is, of course, an alternative and that a better world, one of social justice, is not an unrealizable utopia but a concrete one. The conclusion, and thus the book as a whole, can be seen as a reiteration or an illustration of Gramsci's celebrated principle of the pessimism of reason and the optimism of the will, or as Fredric Jameson has reformulated it, "Cynicism of the Intellect, Utopianism of the Will!" (2010: 13). This alternative or utopia is the ethico-political project that emerges from the critique of Schmitt's notion of politics as the friend-and-enemy logic. On the basis of this notion, Schmitt excludes humanity from the sphere of the political, because humanity supposedly has no enemy. The present book argues that humanity indeed does have an enemy and that it consequently has to constitute itself as a political subject—within a type of politics, however, that is inextricably linked to ethics. The enemy of humanity is the system of oppression and exploitation, domination and alienation, and humiliation and violence represented today by capital in its neoliberal form.

Chapter 1

Ethics and the Law
Reconsidering the Friend-and-Enemy Logic

In one of the most central moments of his *Leviathan*, in chapter 13 of part 1, Thomas Hobbes says, "Where there is no common power, there is no law; where no law, no injustice" (1994: 78). This statement contains the entire logic of political modernity, at least, of the dominant and institutional type of politics grounded in the theory of sovereignty formulated by Hobbes and reaching to our days. For our purposes, what is most important in this statement is the obvious exclusion of ethics from justice and the law and thus from politics. Perhaps the first thing to be noted is that in Hobbes's statement, the final word is not "justice," but "injustice." Although this may at first appear too simplistic, it might be important to also note that had Hobbes said, "Where there is no law, there is no justice," his statement would have been more immediately comprehensible and certainly unproblematic. It would have almost been a tautology, accustomed as we are to thinking of the law in terms of justice, and of justice in terms of the law. By using the word *injustice*, rather than *justice*, Hobbes is simply summing up the theory he has been formulating so far and will continue to formulate in the following chapters of *Leviathan*. He is simply giving an accurate and concise description of that theory based on the notion that the natural condition of humankind is a condition of war—a war of everybody against everybody. In other words, he is saying that if there is no law, anything goes. However, the idea is not that in the absence of the law all kind of injustice can take place. In fact, injustice cannot be committed at all: "Nothing can be unjust" (ibid.). Consequently, there can be no justice either. He says, "The notions of right and wrong, justice and injustice have there no place" (ibid.). Actions and situations are neither just nor unjust; they are what they are.

This is very different from the common idea according to which we need the law, because otherwise, unjust things will easily and frequently happen. In fact, the law itself determines the justness and unjustness of everything, every action and situation. Beyond the law, there is no other way to determine that. Certainly, there is no sense of ethics to distinguish between what is just and unjust, right and wrong. Indeed, there is no ethics at all. If an action is not expressly prohibited by the law, it *can* be performed. In the so-called state of nature, whatever can be done materially belongs in a system of rights that is absolutely open and indeterminate. The limit is only physical, material. For instance, I cannot fly because my nature is so constituted as to not allow that. But I can do everything I can materially do. In the next chapter of *Leviathan*, Hobbes says that "in such a condition, every man has a right to everything, even to one another's body" (80). Obviously, this situation is unsustainable. It is because of this that people come together and decide to give up their rights and enter political society. A contract is made, which establishes the sovereign, and thus the law. From this time on, Hobbes promises, there can be some security and peace. Certainly, the condition of a war of everybody against everybody is overcome. The common power, which is coercive and keeps everybody in awe, will make sure that everybody abides by the law. This will be ensured through a system of punishment and terror (Hobbes is not afraid to use the word *terror* to describe the power of the state and of the law). Without this fear, which the common power instills in everybody's heart, the original condition of war and chaos would persist. It is not because of an innate, instinctual, or natural sense of right and wrong that people respect themselves, the others, and the world. Nor is it because of something like the moral law, which we will see in Kant. There is nothing of the sort. Instead, all is selfish and actually as brutish as the condition of war and violence that needs to be overcome.

The law itself is not the manner in which people try to regulate their life on the basis of their common experience and singularity of needs; rather, it is the original violence of the state of nature institutionalized. The sovereign, who has received everybody's unbridled freedoms and rights, now has the authority to make the law. This law is externally imposed on everybody, superimposed on them. This is truly the extent to which this law can be said to be "common." Otherwise, this common power, which keeps everybody in awe and terror, has nothing *common* about itself. It is the exclusive privilege and right of the sovereign. Moreover, the sovereign cannot commit any injustice, for the sovereign is the only source of the distinction between the just and the unjust. Injustice can be committed against the sovereign; and the greatest form of injustice would obviously be a revolution. But the sovereign can do as he pleases, having—to paraphrase Hobbes—a right to everything, even to everybody's body.

The purpose of this chapter is not simply to give an account, cursory as it might be, of Hobbes's theory of sovereignty and the origin of the political state and the law but to highlight the fact that Hobbes's theory is at work in our society today. The liberal and democratic world—the "free" world—likes to think differently about itself, but in reality at its core we find Hobbes's theory of power, punishment, control, and terror. The implication is not that Hobbes is to be blamed for this. If anything, despite some serious flaws in his theory and some historical blunders, Hobbes is very straightforward and, without any hypocrisy, calls things by their names. He is very adamant about the necessity of a strong coercive power capable of ensuring what is most essential to a functioning society: security. Today we have reached a point of obsession with security. Faced with international (as well as domestic) terrorism, the security of the nation-state seems to be the most urgent aspect of political life. However, differently from Hobbes's clarity and "honesty," we generally like to garb this maniac drive toward a security state with the most beautiful rhetoric about democracy, freedom, and so on. Yet Hobbes was very clear: security entails the loss of all freedom and the implementation of a regime of fear and terror. For him, this was preferable to the chaos and violence of the original state of nature, the state of a war of everybody against everybody. For Hobbes, there was no alternative: either the original chaos and war or the police state of institutional politics and legality, extortion, and terror, which characterizes the modern and contemporary world.

The notion that there is no alternative has become popular with neoliberal policy-makers.[1] The difference is that today instead of saying that there is no alternative to the terror of the security state, to the culture of fear that tries to make everybody obedient and docile, we are told that terror is outside the state of security and constantly threatens it, and fear is mistaken for a sense of prudence and watchfulness. Sovereign power, the true enemy of the common and good life and the true repository of terror, builds an ad hoc enemy in order to justify its sway. Everyday life is turned into a nightmare of apprehension and fear. Gog and Magog (whatever form they might take) are always about to destroy everything—above all, our identity, which is then "patriotic" to defend.

The logic of security, which requires the law as command, works through a manipulation of people's desire. In Hobbes, we find the notion that human beings are machines of desire. In the wonderful introduction to *Leviathan*, he says, "For what is the *heart*, but a *spring*; and the *nerves*, but so many *strings*; and the *joints*, but so many *wheels*, giving motion to the whole body, such as was intended by the artificer?" (3; emphasis in the original). These automata, the work of nature, become the model for that artificial animal, which is the state. In truth, each human being becomes artificial insofar as he or she becomes a political and legal being. It is as if we all had two bodies: a natural body and a legal/political one. Both bodies have power in the most basic sense of having the capacity to do things. This power is also their freedom, and in the case of the natural body, it is also its right. The distinction between the two bodies not only has an analytical function but is also a real distinction. For instance, I may be sick. However, I become a patient only insofar as I seek institutional and medical care. Otherwise, I remain sick without being a patient. Indeed, the paradoxical situation may also obtain where I am a patient without being sick. I am sick insofar as I am a natural body; I become a patient with my legal/political one. The artificial (legal/political) body limits and regulates the natural body. It is characterized by a different form of power and freedom and by the exchange of what Hobbes sees as natural rights with the legal and political rights, which can be granted but can also be taken away. The natural body is unprotected and naked. It is in the condition of bare life. The artificial body is, at least in the tradition originating with Hobbes, subjected to sovereign power.

Early on in the *Leviathan*, in addition to the machine-like aspect of the human body, Hobbes also stresses its never-ending desire, or rather, ending only with death. In this sense, in chapter 11, he takes issue with the "old moral philosophers" (57)—first among them is Aristotle, of course, whom he does not mention—denying that there is such a thing as happiness apart from "a continual progress of the desire, from one object to another, the attaining of the former, being still but the way to the latter" (ibid.). This desire is, most essentially, a desire for power—and for a constant increase of it. This is so important that it becomes a general rule, characteristic of the human condition, or even part of human nature. Hobbes says, "So that in the first place, I put for a general inclination of all mankind, a perpetual and restless desire of power after power, that ceaseth only in death" (58). Hobbes is not speaking here of political power, but of potency. This type of power, the capacity to do things, is necessary to ensure the continuity of one's life situation. An increase of power is necessary to that extent. Hobbes makes this very clear when he says that it "is not always that a man hopes for a more intensive delight than he has already attained to, or that he cannot be content with a moderate power, but because he cannot assure the power and means to live well, which he hath present, without the acquisition of more" (ibid.). On the one hand, we might detect here the ideology of incessant growth typical of modernity and capital; on the other, however, we can also understand that the work of maintenance itself requires an increase of power, a desire for more. So far, we have a materialist philosophy with which it is easy to agree. The point, however, is that among the many desires—and one that will become dominant—we also find the desire for security and peace. This is unproblematic in and of itself. Anyone may readily recognize how realistic it is for people to desire a situation in which—as Hobbes says in one of the most quoted pages from chapter 13 of *Leviathan*—they do not have to be constantly under "continual fear, and danger of violent death," living "without other security than what their own strength and their own invention shall furnish them withal" (76). What is problematic is the solution that Hobbes gives to this problem. "Leviathan" is the name for this solution. In the either-or situation described by Hobbes, people exchange the original fear and violence of the state of nature for the institutional and sovereign terror of the political state. It is in this sense that the coming law is nothing but the original violence "refined" and institutionalized. Living in a security state is not the same as having actual existential security. As we will see in some of the next chapters, very often this formal and institutional security becomes insecurity for large sections of any given population, and in the age of globalization, it becomes global insecurity. The desire for security and peace is betrayed and replaced by the objectivity of a control or disciplinary machine, by the system of the police, and the network of surveillance. This is the way in which desire is manipulated and sidetracked. The artificial animals—the automata—that now populate the greater artificial animal (i.e., the state, the great Leviathan) represent, as Hobbes says in chapter 18 of part 2, "the confusion of a disunited multitude" (111) now united as a people and subjected to the sovereign. Desire, a subjective condition, is lost in the objectification of all subjectivities, all singularities. The desire of power and the power itself are transferred to the person of the sovereign; they become the sovereign's exclusive privilege, and the sovereign becomes the only recognizable and recognized singularity.

I want to mention at least two problems in Hobbes's account of the origin of political society and the law. One has to do with the transition from the state of nature to the state of political society. The former is a condition in which there is precisely "no society" (76) and thus nothing recognizably human. If we think, for instance, of Aristotle's well-known notion that the human being is a political animal by nature, we see that being political, or social, and being human can be understood as identical. The absence of the political is the absence of the human. So much so that, parenthetically, when we are told today to leave politics out of the workplace, we are being dehumanized. Hobbes is saying the exact opposite of Aristotle, since for him there is a *passage* to political society, which is different from the natural condition. The human being is certainly an animal by nature, yet not a political one. This political dimension is artificial, not in the sense that it is fake or inauthentic, but in the sense that it is made. It is made *by art*—namely, labor and doing. It is a transformation of the original nature. Yet it is difficult to understand how these prepolitical (and thus prehuman) beings may come to grasp the benefits of leaving their natural condition behind and entering the political state. Even assuming the clarity and strength of their absolutely selfish motives, how can they arrive at the notion of a contract? It is true that for Hobbes the natural condition is only a hypothesis— though he also says that it is found in actual reality (and it is here that he commits his historical blunder, as we will see next). Yet the transition to political society and the law is not explained at all, not even at the hypothetical level. It is not explained because it cannot be. It remains pure fiction and, in truth, a flaw. It is probably much better to say, with Aristotle, that the political is natural. In other words, with respect to humanity, there is nothing prepolitical, and thus prehuman. Of course, the human being is not the only political/social animal. Nor is it important to assess the extent of this political aspect for the human animal or other nonhuman ones. Rather, what is important, in the human context, is the type of politics that is being made. Hobbes only gives us a politics completely devoid of ethics. The law as command, which is the essence of the political for Hobbes, establishes the just and the unjust, as we have seen. Beyond that horizon, beyond the legal and political frame, we only have the brutish condition of nature, which is really difficult to call human—even by Hobbes's own standards. Perhaps "there was never such a time . . . as this" (77), Hobbes insinuates, or was there?

It is at this point that we find Hobbes's enormous historical blunder, or perhaps an outright historical false-hood. Hobbes says, "It may peradventure be thought, there was never such a time nor condition of war as this; and I believe it was never generally so, over all the world. But there are many places, where they live so now. For the savage people of many places of *America* (except the government of small families, the concord whereof depen-deth on natural lust) have no government at all and live at this day in that brutish manner as I said before" (ibid.). We are in the midst of the conquest: that genocidal his-tory that began with the so-called age of discovery and continues to the present day. We know today that the *sav-age* people of America who lived in that *brutish* manner in fact had a much better way of life and of govern-ing themselves and preserving the balance of the earth than the Europeans, especially in the age of the emergence of the nation-state, sovereignty, and modernity (i.e., mod-ern politics and the modern law). However, these lines should not be taken as a perhaps inessential illustration of what the chaotic, anarchic state of nature, the war of everybody against everybody, might be in actual his-torical reality. What Hobbes is doing here is providing (a) a substantiation of his argument for a strong, coercive government—namely, a common power that keeps every-body under a regime of fear and terror (for "natural lust" is evidently not sufficient to keep communities together)—and (b) a justification for European genocidal policies in the newly "discovered" lands, in the "lost" worlds, or in the occupied territories. We can then go back to our initial Hobbes quote: "Where there is no common power, there is no law; where no law, no injustice." The fact

that there was, among the indigenous people of the Amer-
icas, no recognizable (in the Europeans' eyes) common
power, no government apart from that of small families,
which was based on natural lust rather than on law, implied
that no injustice could be committed against them. At
the same time, where a common power was found, it was
readily destroyed and the people protected or oppressed
by that common power were brought back to the original
state of war, of bare life. This type of thinking and acting
continued throughout the centuries of conquest, the history of colonialism and imperialism, and it continues today
as well. Iraq is a perfect example of this, and more recently,
Libya. According to this type of thinking, either there is
no recognizable common power and thus all is permissible
or the existent common power (today named ad hoc a
"rogue state") is overthrown in order to make everything
permissible. Here I am going beyond Hobbes in order to
establish a link to the friend-and-enemy logic prepared by
his thought. Indeed, the history of sovereignty is a history
of identity, the making of identity, which occurs through
violence. That means that the construction of a sovereign nation always implies the subjection or annihilation
of other singularities: the construction of identity and the
annihilation of difference. What is perceived as different
becomes a danger, a threat: it is the enemy, which must
be destroyed. The issue is obviously that of security. The
security, not simply of a sovereign nation but of the sovereignty paradigm as a whole (i.e., the paradigm of the
law as order and as command), is called into question by
the presence of situations that resist it, say, communities
organized (for Hobbes) on natural lust. When enmity, and
thus war, occurs among sovereign states, there is always
a process whereby the difference of the other is seen as a
problem and thus as a determining factor. If it is not natural lust, it has to be something similar to it—certainly a
trait of inferiority, ferocity, and so on. This usually goes

under the name of dehumanization of the enemy, a process that can be more or less explicit and conscious.

This process of dehumanization is different from what Carl Schmitt claims about the political enemy. However, the question is whether his claim is convincing and correct. For Schmitt, politics is the relationship of friend and enemy. In saying this, more strongly than ever in the history of Western political thought, he establishes the autonomy of the political—autonomy from any other sphere of life but particularly from ethics. A precondition for such autonomy is that the enemy be considered a political, rather than personal, enemy. As such, the enemy is not dehumanized but is actually worthy of respect.

Schmitt goes back to the Latin and Greek words for the distinction between the political and personal enemy. He says, "The enemy is not merely any competitor or just any partner of a conflict in general. He is also not the private adversary whom one hates. An enemy exists only when, at least potentially, one fighting collectivity of people confronts a similar collectivity" (Schmitt 1996: 28). In other words, the true enemy is only political, or as Schmitt says, the "enemy is solely the public enemy" (ibid.). He explains the difference between the two notions: "The enemy is *hostis*, not *inimicus* in the broader sense; πολέμιος, not ἐχθρός" (ibid.).

Schmitt employs a very technical notion of the enemy. Indeed, it would be a very good thing if he were right. The true enemy would only be the public enemy, the enemy of the state, with whom a war might break out but also be avoided. The relationship with the enemy would be one without passions, feelings, and emotions. According to this notion, I might hate my neighbor, a person I know, an acquaintance, a relative, and so on. Even a friend can at one point become my personal enemy. But this would not be the true or political enemy. The latter is simply any citizen belonging to a country with which my own country is at war—potentially or actually. I really have no reason to hate this person, whom I do not even know. It is not a question of love and hate, sympathy or antipathy. The emotions have nothing to do with the definition of the political enemy. Schmitt says, "The enemy in the political sense need not be hated personally, and in the private sphere only does it make sense to love one's enemy, i.e., one's adversary" (29). This might seem puzzling at first. Its meaning is in fact the autonomy of the political. Schmitt makes this statement after quoting from the New Testament, the "often quoted 'Love your enemies'" (ibid.). Still referring to the Latin and Greek distinction between the private and public enemy, Schmitt says that it is only the former (the private or personal enemy) that is meant here. Schmitt's paragraph ends with this very interesting sentence, "It [i.e., the Bible quotation] does not mean that one should love and support the enemies of one's own people" (ibid.).

There are many important points coming together here. One is the implicit idea of *aiding the enemy*—namely, the idea that this is an absolute wrong. We know that formally the enemy is understood as any citizen of a country with which your country is at war. Aiding the enemy is wrong, and in fact it is a crime, punishable by law. It does not matter what the circumstances are or who the enemy is (e.g., the type of relationship you might have with him or her). It is a political, not a personal, question. Indeed, it is for Schmitt the political question par excellence. The enemy should not be supported or loved just as he or she should not be hated either. In the political type of antagonism, which is "the most intense and extreme antagonism" (ibid.), the enemy should be vanquished and destroyed— yet all this should happen without the involvement of any moral or psychological aspect. This is why I spoke of a very technical notion of the enemy in Schmitt.

It is perhaps important to draw the general scheme of Schmitt's philosophy. Interestingly, there is some formal similarity with Kant's ethical thought, which I will discuss in the final pages of this chapter. Simply put, in Kant we have the autonomy of ethics, of the moral and rational will; in Schmitt, we have the autonomy of the political, of a very rational and political will. But the similarity is only formal, for in terms of content we are led toward very different ends. What is certain is that Kant's concept of autonomy, because of its universality, is more compelling than Schmitt's. Indeed, the autonomy of the political, seen from Schmitt's definition of the political itself, as the relationship of friend and enemy, needs to be particularistic in nature. Universality, as we will see in a moment discussing the concept of humanity, is excluded from it. Thus Schmitt can say, "Never in the thousand-year struggle between Christians and Moslems did it occur to a Christian to surrender rather than defend Europe out of love toward the Saracens or Turks" (ibid.). Beside the question of the historical accuracy of this statement, it might be important to ask the ontological question of identity, of what makes one a Christian or a Muslim, and so on. The answer is nothing but circumstances. The ontology in question is of course of a historical, political, and existential type. The next question would then be, "What happens to the humanity of the Christian, the Muslim, and so on?" This is the question that Schmitt's philosophy could not answer and is in truth not even interested in posing. Yet it is a very important question, unless we assume that the identities necessary to the friend-and-enemy political logic—be they of a religious, ethnic, national, or any other type—are unsurpassable, metaphysical categories of human life.

Before speaking about the notion of humanity, I need to point out how Schmitt's theory is and is not functional to the real world today. It is insofar as the concept of the enemy is a central—if not the most central—concept in

the harmful and corrupt "grand politics" that is leading the world toward the abyss; it is not insofar as the
enemy is systematically construed as the evil and hateful
one—and this is contrary to Schmitt's main precept. My
claim is that this is because Schmitt's distinction between
the personal (or private) and the political (or public)
enemy is fundamentally a false one, because the enemy
(whether private or public) cannot be construed in a pas-
sionless manner, and because the political does not have
the autonomy Schmitt argues it has but is on the contrary
univocal with that which Schmitt's theory excludes from
it—namely, humanity. The friend-and-enemy theory leads
not to the formation of a political consciousness, where
politics is necessarily tied to ethics (i.e., to a sense of a
just society and the good life for all) but rather to ossified
political identities, such as nations, states, religions, and so
on. When individuals identify themselves with these categories, ideological distortions do the rest, justifying in
their eyes the most violent actions and situations all for the
sake of defending those identities. Something like "aiding
the enemy" is made up and seen as aberrant: a betrayal or
treason. The enemy is always defined by the identity that
excludes it. It is never a human being.

The whole notion of aiding the enemy is a legal and narrowly political notion, not sustained by ethics. As we will
see in the section on Antigone in chapter 2, this is a very
problematic notion. The question is, "Who is the (public)
enemy?" It could be my own brother, just as is the case in
Antigone. But it is precisely in cases like this that the inad-
equacy of Schmitt's distinction becomes clear. Contrary to
what Schmitt thinks, a process of dehumanization is always
involved in the making of the enemy. But one more time,
the point is perhaps to overcome the enemy thought and
find a new humanity in the place of the friend-and-enemy
game. In sum, politics is not defined by the relationship
of friend and enemy, which is quite vague, but rather

by the relationship of oppressor and oppressed, whose destruction and overcoming entail an ethico-political project.[2]

Schmitt's political thinking must be understood from the perspective of the logic of total war. This does not mean that Schmitt *favors* war, but simply that war "must . . . remain a real possibility for as long as the concept of the enemy remains valid" (33). One may ask for how long. The answer would have to be for as long as there is political society. Schmitt says, "A world in which the possibility of war is utterly eliminated, a completely pacified globe, would be a world without distinction of friend and enemy and hence a world without politics" (35). As is often the case with Schmitt, we have here a thought that implodes and repeats itself. In fact, politics, the friend-and-enemy distinction, and war are ultimately one and the same thing. Perhaps what Schmitt fails to show is why the absence of all this would be a problem. As I have previously noted, he works from a very technical viewpoint, and his interest is limited to the definition of the political. From such a point of view, he says, it is "even irrelevant whether such a world without politics is desirable as an ideal situation" (ibid.). However, if the question is not a technical one, if it is not a question of *defining* the political but rather seeing it as a means to the good life and living it as a way to a just world, then the notion of humanity becomes central. For Schmitt, this would be a complete absurdity. He says, "Humanity is not a political concept" (55). For Schmitt, it *is not* because it cannot be and because "no political entity or society and no status corresponds to it" (ibid.). This of course follows from his technical, narrow definition of the political. In *The Concept of the Political*, there are two important statements supporting this claim: (1) "Humanity as such cannot wage war because it has no enemy, at least not on this planet" and (2) "the concept of humanity excludes the concept of the enemy, because the enemy does not cease to be a human being" (1996: 54). These two statements, however, can lead to completely different conclusions from the ones Schmitt draws. In fact, instead of excluding the concept of humanity from the political sphere and separating politics from ethics, we can see here the need for overcoming the enemy thought altogether. In other words, the problem should not be humanity but the enemy, that is to say, the logic of the enemy and of war.

For Schmitt, the political is only a special sector, rather than the very fabric, of the social, of everyday life and humanity. This also describes well the situation we find throughout the world today at the institutional level. The political class of any country has its own special interests, and it is usually taken for granted that this is the way it should be. People's everyday life, their humanity, and their troubles and fragility are mere matter under the domination of a self-appointed and self-defined class claiming a privileged access and a right to authority within the political sphere. This is not to say that Schmitt's theory is responsible for this state of affairs, but rather that it represents one of the clearest theoretical descriptions of our present condition. However, this is a condition that goes beyond Schmitt, and as Giorgio Agamben (1998) shows in *Homo Sacer* and other works, it has to do with the separation between sovereign power and naked life, reaching its most mature stage in our age of biopolitics and biopower, where all life becomes the matter of political representation and domination. Although Schmitt is a theoretician of the absolutist, dictatorial state, our so-called representative, parliamentary democracies today are nothing but more sophisticated forms of dictatorship. In their professed liberal ideology, we find an abuse of the theories of thinkers like Hobbes and Schmitt. The difference is that such theories, perhaps formulated in earnest by these thinkers, are now applied in the most hypocritical way—and that also means the cruelest yet most efficient way. The political class worldwide, taking advantage of the false legitimacy of the notion of politics as a separate sphere, dominating life in its most diverse manifestations, is made of people who misappropriate and abuse their otherwise miserable power, grounded in violence or the threat thereof. This is a class of people that must be completely eliminated. That does not mean, of course, physically eliminating the people belonging to that class, but rather eliminating the class itself as a possibility in political life and letting these people do something useful to the world instead of taking advantage of and indeed destroying it. The system itself must be reformed so that humanity might become the subject of a new type of politics rather than its raw material. The notion of reform should not be taken in the usual, technical sense of the stale politics that must be demolished but rather in the political-ontological sense of a new formation, a transformation, which must be radical and revolutionary.

In denying humanity any political status, Schmitt over-looks the fact that humanity too often becomes the enemy of a political system that—in order to sustain itself in its false autonomy and in order to reiterate and reinforce its illegitimate authority and power—is willing to annihilate it altogether. This is obviously the case with the political system that we identify as capitalism. The point, then, is for humanity to constitute itself as a political subject, become aware of this uncalled-for enmity, and act accordingly. The elimination of this system of violence seems to be the only solution to the age of despair and "crisis" we live in, the only alternative to the approaching end of humanity itself.

A new type of politics, grounded in ethics, needs to conceive of humanity as a political concept and a political subject. We have seen that for Schmitt this is impossible because humanity has no enemy and consequently cannot wage a war, which is for Schmitt the precondition of the political. He is of course quite right in saying that when

the notion of humanity is invoked by a state fighting its
political enemy, we have a problem. In fact, what today
is often called "humanitarian intervention" "is not a war
for the sake of humanity, but a war wherein a particular
state seeks to *usurp* a universal concept against its military
opponent" (1996: 54; emphasis added). This happens all
the time, and it is so true that it also makes us realize the
pure and formal technicality of Schmitt's position. Despite
his political realism, he remains a very idealist thinker. In
truth, the political enemy always also becomes a personal
and moral enemy: the quintessence of evil. For Schmitt,
when this happens, we have a misuse, an abuse, and usurpation of a universal concept. He is very adamant about the
dangers of this position, which is the most usual and common position in today's world. He says, "To confiscate the
word humanity, to invoke and monopolize such a term
probably has certain incalculable effects, such as denying
the enemy the quality of being human and declaring him to
be an outlaw of humanity; and a war can thereby be driven
to the most extreme inhumanity" (ibid.). Yes, quite right.
However, Schmitt overlooks the fact that an ongoing war
against humanity is waged by the system of economic and
political power at many levels, and that it has many aspects:
from the war that empire, and the various imperial or
quasi-imperial states, wages against historically oppressed
people; to the class war in any given nation as well as globally; and again to the war that every system of power (with
its army, bureaucracy, and police) wages against people in
their everyday lives. If this is true, then humanity does
have an enemy. Notably, in our modernity, the system of
capital *is* the enemy of humanity. We often say that it is an
inhuman (or inhumane) system. Indeed, here the priva-
tive prefix *in*-means the denial, crippling, or destruction of
humanity. To be sure, it is Schmitt himself who provides
some insight in this respect. In an interesting footnote to
the earlier-quoted passage, he shows how "the Indians of

North America" were exterminated precisely on the moral
ground of a supposed lack of humanity (they were accused
of eating human flesh). Schmitt notes, "As civilization pro-
gresses and morality rises, even less harmless things than
devouring human flesh could perhaps qualify as deserving
to be outlawed in such a manner. Maybe one day it will be
enough if a people were unable to pay its debts" (54–55,
note 23). Indeed, we have already reached that "one day,"
for today, in the age of financial capital, being in debt represents the condition of radical inhumanity for a growing
number of people all over the world: their dehumanization. It also represents, as Maurizio Lazzarato (2012)
argues, the new configuration of the class struggle. Back
to Schmitt, I only want to note that his use of the word
moral or *morality* has nothing to do with my use of the
word "ethics" or with Kant's notion of the moral law I will
be discussing later. Schmitt understands morality only as
a cultural system of moralistic norms and habits, and that
is completely different from the universal and common
ethics required for the construction of a just world. This
type of ethics is already political—namely, linked to the
science of the community and the project of the good life.
This is indeed what belongs essentially to humanity and
what defines it. Only by recuperating its political status
can humanity, which is essentially an ethical *and* political concept, deactivate and destroy the inhuman system
of domination and violence bent on its destruction. The
question of the place of those (the elites and their guards)
who support this system of violence and thus profit from
it is easily explained. They are the saddest and most miserable human beings who take advantage of a system that is
not necessarily in their favor and may turn against them
at any time. They have no sense of ethics and choose one
or another form of violence to defend their particularistic
and petty interests. Even their politics can only equivocally
be called so; for in forsaking humanity (the humanity in

them), they also renounce the true sense of the political as a means for the good life for their community and for all. The problem is not their physical existence but the conditions for its possibility. These conditions are within the system of violence itself, and it is there that a change must be brought about. It is true—as Machiavelli says—that in the world there are two classes of people: those who want to dominate and those who do not want to be dominated.[3] He adds that the latter are of course closer to freedom. However, even the former are nothing without the relations of domination and violence proper to the system as such. Without those relations, they are forced to correct their pathological desire, their cynicism, and debauchery. Without the *pathological law*,[4] which protects their interests, these people would see the end of their supposed autonomy—namely, their "right" to conquer and plunder.

The friend-and-enemy logic is a silly—though extremely dangerous—ideological construct, and the fact that it has acquired such currency and importance in human history is mind-boggling. Saddam Hussein, the friend, becomes the worst enemy. However, what is the status of the people of Iraq in this logic? What is, in a particularly tragic moment of this insane war, the status of children in the city of Fallujah who are still being born with horrific, unnatural birth defects after the brutal US attacks on the city in 2004?[5] Do they count as friends or as enemies? Probably, in the logic of politics as war, they do not count at all. They are part of what goes under the name of collateral damage. They were, in any case, disposable beings to begin with. Some "humanitarian" assistance will set the record right and, above all, put our conscience at ease. After all, politics is politics, and war is war. What is important is that the friend-and-enemy logic remains in order to keep the system of power (the "balance" of power) intact and going—truly, a system of oppression and unimaginable violence.

In truth, behind its ideological mask, the friend-and-enemy logic is the struggle between the oppressors and the oppressed (i.e., the class struggle). It is this struggle that brings about, often unlikely, alliances and enmities. The will of the oppressors to continue and increase their oppression and the resistance of the oppressed intending to end the oppression so that they may make time and space for a dignified life are the basic elements of what then appears to be as a split between enemies and friends. The people of a nation at war with another have traditionally no interest whatsoever in the course of the conflict. They very often do not even know what the real problem is and why they should be fighting. It is only because of the power of ideologies—for instance, nationalism—that they may come to distinguish between friends (their own people) and enemies (the other people). However, they know very well that this is false. Those that they call enemies are completely unknown to them; among those that they call friends they find their most brutal oppressors. Without the ideologies of identity, most notably nationalism and patriotism (but also ethnic and religious identities), the struggle would be determined by the material conditions of life; it would only be a struggle of the oppressed against the oppressors for the elimination of the system of oppression as such and the constitution of an ethically just, and a politically functional, world. The determination of the oppressors to maintain their power is perhaps the most important element in the construction of those ideologies. They are ideologies lacking in universality and reflecting this or that particularistic interest, and as such, they are *pathological* in Kant's sense of the word. They lack any true sense of ethics and only express *moral fanaticism* or *fanaticism* in general, which Kant defines as "a deliberate overstepping of the limits of human reason" (1996: 107).

Moral fanaticism is an overstepping of ethical reason (for Kant, practical pure reason). Ethical reason "forbids us to place the subjective determining principle of correct actions, that is, their real *motive*, in anything but the law itself" (ibid.). This is of course not what Kant calls pathological law but moral or practical law based on a rational (i.e., universal) sense of duty, which "strikes down all *arrogance* as well as vain *self-love*" (ibid.).

Instead, pathological law is the law as command, handled by the state, its bureaucracy and police. It is the law that is not based on universal and human principles of freedom and dignity but rather on the defense of particularistic interests, the security of a selected and privileged class of people capable of assuming the role of sovereign through violence. It is the law that protects the right to private property—that is, to privatize or to take away from people what is common; dispossess and displace them; and force them to leave their homes and places of origin, migrate, and find themselves at the mercy of all types of despotic power, violence, exploitation, and humiliation. This law is nothing but violence institutionalized. It is a self-legitimizing situation that has no true legitimacy whatsoever. Its alleged legitimacy and authority rest on the prison and the gun. An example is when a rightful demonstration is met by the brutality of the police, an all-too-frequent occurrence, and demonstrators are beaten, jailed, and tortured. The term *justice* associated with this type of law is used in a highly equivocal way. In truth, the aim of pathological law is the production of injustice for the maintenance of division within societies and of the status quo.

An altogether different law is what Kant calls moral or practical law. Its most characteristic feature is the universalizing principle that sharply separates it from the pathological sphere of particular interests and selfish desire. Its universal scope is what many see as a problem, for it seems that, because of this, it cannot account for the difference that one necessarily finds in experience. In other words, how can the law apply univocally in all situations everywhere? However, for Kant—this is his categorical imperative—what must be universalized is not the action but the maxim (the principle or reason) of the action. Thus it is the disposition that must be universal. An action has ethical worth only insofar as its maxim can become universal. Of course, any action is particular; it occurs here and now. An action cannot be universalized. Even if I repeat the same action tomorrow, it will be a different one. Yet its principle can be universalized. For instance, refraining from doing harm is a universal principle, regardless of the particular situation in which harm may or may not happen; respecting other people's dignity and autonomy is also another universal principle, and one does not have to know the details or particulars of a situation in order to follow and uphold it. Even from these simple examples, it is clear how this type of law is completely different from the one that comes from the decision of the sovereign, detached from the body politic and pursuing its own interests or following its own whim. In the obligation (or duty) that comes with the moral law, sovereignty is no longer necessary. Universal practical principles—namely, the disposition with which anyone ought to act—do not need the state to enforce them. These principles do not of course say whether one ought to eat or not eat this type of food, dress or not dress in any specific way, engage or not engage in any specific sexual act, and so on. In fact, the choice of the particular action to be performed is a matter not of ethics but rather of cultural values and norms, which change from place to place and time to time. Cultures, like languages, are all different from one another—none of them is superior or inferior to the others; they are all equally beautiful, interesting, and complex, but they have nothing to do with ethics. Similarly, there is nothing ethical or not ethical about wearing or not wearing a certain garment. Indeed, those who say the opposite do not know what they are talking about. Their views are moralistic, and truly pathological, but they are not ethical. Obviously, according to the friend-and-enemy logic, these particulars become very important. The enemy is the one who dresses in such and such a way, eats food that should not be eaten, engages in sexual acts that are against nature, and so on. But the triviality and falsity of these types of judgments is evident to anyone who is willing to think. Sovereignty and identity require that these false notions be defended. Ethics, in contrast, requires the dismantling of sovereignty itself, and even of identity. It can tolerate anything (and tolerance is indeed one of its most essential traits), but it cannot tolerate that the nonethical should prevail.

Ethics is, for Kant, found in the kingdom of ends—which is really no kingdom at all. Here the pathological law has no bearing whatsoever. Instead, one finds dignity and freedom. Everybody here is a legislator, meaning that no state and no police need to dictate the law. However, everybody legislates according to the same universal principles and practical laws. In other words, the true legislator is the moral law itself—that is to say, ethics. Everybody stands under the same ethical principles, though everybody will perform different actions and be involved in different situations. But the schematism is the same, and one has accepted it willingly; in fact, it is ultimately a subjective choice to stand under and respect the moral law. Everybody legislates, but no one is above the law or at the borderline (which is the place of the sovereign for Schmitt). This is what Kant says in *Grounding for the Metaphysics of Morals*, "A rational being belongs to the kingdom of ends as a member when he legislates in it universal laws while also being himself subject to these laws" (1981: 40). It is true that in the next sentence he uses the word *sovereign*: "He belongs to it as a sovereign, when as legislator he is himself subject to the will of no other" (ibid.). However, as I will show in a moment with a reference to the *Critique of Practical Reason*, this should not be taken too literally. Probably, what Kant means here is simply the fact that the pathological law is gone and no other person's or agency's will is imposed on anyone. So contrary to what might appear to be the case, we precisely have the elimination of sovereignty. Indeed, if everybody is a sovereign, no one needs to be.

In the *Critique of Practical Reason*, Kant makes it clear that, in achieving freedom, sovereignty is gone. He says, "We are indeed legislative members of a moral kingdom *rendered possible by freedom*, and presented to us by reason as an object of respect; but yet we are subjects in it, not the sovereign" (1996: 103; emphasis added). If there is a sovereign, that is the moral law. However, even this is not truly the case, for the paradigm of sovereignty no longer applies here. We are talking about something completely different from it. Indeed, the command of the moral law is not the same as the sovereign command because first of all, and perhaps in the most trivial sense, there is no police or military retaliation and no punishment for not following the moral law. The command is objective, but the decision to follow or not follow the law, to be ethical or not, is a subjective one. The law here is nothing but another name for humanity, not for the separation characteristic of the paradigm of sovereignty. Humanity here is not an abstraction, but it is concrete; it does not have a price, thus a quantifiable value, but it has dignity, which is quality, not quantity. Dignity is "above price, and therefore admits of no equivalent" (1981: 40). In a previous work, I spoke in this sense of the *dignity of individuation* (Gullì 2010), which can and should really be broadened beyond the realm of humanity. But even if we stay for a moment within the limits of the human context, we can appreciate the fact that each individuating and individuated existence has an irreplaceable dignity. This is the truth of ethics and of what we know as human rights, which have had a terrible adventure to this date but should be redirected to their legitimate source. From this point of view, it makes no sense to speak of friend and enemy. However, this does not mean that it makes no sense to speak politically; rather, we ought to do so, but with the awareness that politics without ethics is worthless and even dangerous. Ethics points to dignity, and dignity does not point to the friend-and-enemy divide but to the struggle between the oppressor and the oppressed, which is at one and the same time an ethical and political struggle. Furthermore (and I will go back to this in Chapter 5), the ethics of dignity—but there cannot be another ethics—counters violence. This is not to say that it is merely reactive. This *countering*, which is necessarily political, comes from dignity's original place and disposition—a place of resistance and a disposition toward happiness and the good life. This is perhaps what in other terminology could be referred to as natural and inalienable rights, which each individuating dignity has to begin with. In other words, each human being—but truly each being (whether human or nonhuman)—occupies this place in the cosmos and has this disposition. It can be, and it is, trampled on. Oppression is of course a reality and brutality and violence are very common and on the rise. The task of the ethics and politics of dignity, which is an immense yet invaluable task, is to counter and zero out this tendency and this reality.

MACHIAVELLI AND THE DESIRE OF FREEDOM

In a section of what in the English *Selections from the Prison Notebooks* is called "The Modern Prince," a section titled "Prediction and Perspective," perhaps the most interesting section from a philosophical point of view, Antonio

Gramsci deals with Niccolò Machiavelli's notion of effective reality (*la verità effettuale della cosa*) and the difference between what *is* and what *ought to be*. Machiavelli's idea is that the prince, and thus everybody, in order to be successful and avoid destruction and ruin, should focus on what is rather than on what ought to be. One should focus on effective reality. This is usually understood as Machiavelli's political realism.

In *The Prince*, the idea of effective reality is perhaps the most important. It is the idea whereby Machiavelli is seen as a political scientist—that is, the thinker who opens the way to the autonomy of the political; certainly, the thinker who sharply distinguishes between politics and ethics. Moreover, at first sight, Machiavelli would be a thinker who has no concern for political ontology but only looks at what is there—the political given—and offers a description, an anatomy, of it. Indeed, he also offers a prescription only insofar as the prince must follow the dictates of the real, effective reality and of what is. In truth, things stand very differently, and Gramsci shows that very well. Effective reality includes possibility, potentiality, and contingency. What *is* is also what *could be*.

The passage to which Gramsci refers in the aforementioned note on Machiavelli is from chapter 15 of *The Prince*. It is a famous passage in which Machiavelli says,

> But my hope is to write a book that will be useful, at least to those who read it intelligently, and so I thought it sensible to go straight to *a discussion of how things are in real life* [verità effettuale della cosa] and not waste time with a discussion of an imaginary world. For many authors have constructed imaginary republics and principalities that have never existed in practice and never could; for the gap between how people actually behave and how they ought to behave is so great that anyone who ignores everyday reality in order to live up to an ideal will soon discover he has been taught how to destroy himself, not how to preserve himself. (1995: 48; emphasis and brackets added)

Machiavelli is speaking against the imaginary and ideal (something like the utopia that Thomas More had later published in 1516), but what is his view about the concrete possibility contained in what already *is?*

For Gramsci, the political realism contained in this passage, as well as in *The Prince* as a whole, should not make us think of Machiavelli as someone who is merely interested in what is there—that is, effective reality understood as excluding potentiality. The opposite is the case: the potential and possible are equally constitutive elements of effective reality, of "how things are in real life" (according to the translation I am using). Indeed, in real life things might not be what they ought to be, but their very being opens up to and includes what could be. What is important is that the possible be understood in its concrete and material reality.

For Gramsci, Machiavelli is not a diplomat or a mere scientist who has to keep within the limits of effective reality, which is understood as what is merely visible and tangible and what is there in front of us and limits us. Indeed, Machiavelli is *a poet*. Gramsci does not use this word but he uses the word *creator*, which in this sense (a Vichian sense, if you will) is the same. Gramsci begins by saying, "But Machiavelli is not merely a scientist: he is a partisan, a man of powerful passions, an active politician, who wishes to create a new balance of forces and therefore cannot help concerning himself with what 'ought to be' (*not of course in a moralistic sense*)" (1971: 172; emphasis added). Soon, Gramsci will clearly say that there are two concepts of what ought to be. Machiavelli is of course not interested in the moralistic concept. So in what way does he concern himself with it? In other words, what is the concept of *what ought to be* that Machiavelli is interested in? Gramsci does not say. He does not use the words *ontological* and *ethical*. He does stress, however, that the concept of what ought to be—that is, the concept with which Machiavelli concerns himself (despite the passage I read from chapter 15 of *The Prince* in which he says that the ruler must look at what is)—has a political, historical, realistic, and concrete dimension. Obviously, Gramsci is right. This is indeed what interests Machiavelli; certainly not an unreal and fantastic situation, which *is* not, but moralistically, ought to be. Yet insofar as this is true, Machiavelli is really concerned with political ontology (i.e., the constitution of the political and social world) and thus with ethics—that is, ethics that is not moralistic thinking to be sure (and Gramsci is absolutely correct in this). Why ethics? Because what ought to be is, as Gramsci says, "concrete will" (1971: 390) and the will transports the whole discussion to the plane of ethics and, in particular, the plane of contingency and human freedom—namely, of what can be and not be. So more than speaking of two concepts of what ought to be, it would be better to distinguish between what ought to be and what could be. Machiavelli knows very well that the latter (i.e., the possible and potential) is part of effective reality properly understood; it is part of what is. It is, in other words, a concrete tendency within that reality—one that *could* unfold and develop, though it could also not do so. Indeed, there is no intrinsic necessity that it should and no certainty that it will. But there is concrete clarity as to the fact that it could, that *there is an alternative*—contrary to a thinking that becomes specific in our neoliberal times.

Gramsci says Machiavelli "bases himself on effective reality, but what is this effective reality?" (And this is Gramsci's own question). Gramsci's answer, in the form of a further question, a rhetorical question, points to potentiality. He asks, is this effective reality "something static and immobile, or is it not rather a relation of forces in continuous motion and shift of equilibrium?" (ibid.). Obviously, the latter is the case. Thus effective reality (what is) includes *the will to creation*, the "will to the creation of a new equilibrium," on the basis of tendencies and forces present and operative in the old one. Effective reality includes becoming, or coming to be. When one is involved in the effort of creation in this way, according to Gramsci, "one still moves on the terrain of effective reality, but does so in order to dominate and transcend it (or contribute to this)" (ibid.). At this point, Gramsci can highlight the fundamental aspects of Machiavelli's political ontology, which are interestingly based on what Machiavelli seems to reject at first sight: the dimension or modality of what ought to be—namely, the potential and the possible. In fact, it is this modality that precisely is concrete, realistic, historical, political, *and* ethical. Thus Gramsci says, "What 'ought to be' is therefore concrete; indeed, it is the only realistic and historicist interpretation of reality, it alone is history in the making and philosophy in the making, it alone is politics" (ibid.). Becoming, potentiality, and possibility, we all recognize these concepts in the passage by Gramsci I just quoted. What we have here is a full ontology of contingency, of what can be and not be, and thus a full theory of ethics, the practical science of freedom, part of political science, as Aristotle holds.

I have already said how there are, for Gramsci, "two concepts of what ought to be: the abstract and phantasmagorical concept of Savonarola [the prophetic and moralistic friar who denounces all corruption], and the realistic concept of Machiavelli—realistic even if it did not in fact become direct reality, since one cannot expect an individual or a book to change reality but only to interpret it and to indicate the possible lines of action" (172–173; brackets added).

I have also said how I prefer the modality of "what could be" than "what ought to be" when speaking of Machiavelli, as well as in general. And I would venture to say that this is indeed what Gramsci means, what he is talking about. Interestingly, he says that perhaps this "realistic" ought to be will not become "direct reality." Is perhaps Gramsci not saying—and I am of course thinking here of categories typically employed by Agamben—that there is a possibility that such a potentiality will not pass into actuality? In other words, is Gramsci not speaking about contingency—namely, the full formula of freedom, which includes potentiality and the potentiality-not-to? Is he not speaking ontologically, politically, and ethically, addressing that which can be and not be (i.e., the dynamic interplay of fortune and virtue in the constitution of political reality)? What is certain is that Machiavelli's project is realistic and historical (historicist, says Gramsci) precisely because reality is not reduced by him to what merely is, the merely given, but it essentially includes what can be and what could be.

I will now focus on another extremely important moment of Machiavelli's political ontology. This is intimately related to the idea of effective reality (of what is) and points to the freedom of potentiality (of what could be, which always implies the potentiality-not-to and also what could not be). I am referring to a passage from chapter 15 of *The Prince*, where Machiavelli says that "in every city one finds . . . two opposed classes," the people and the elite. He continues saying that these two classes "are at odds because the people do not want to be dominated or oppressed by the elite; and the elite want to dominate and oppress the people" (1995: 31).[6] After dismissing the possibility of a healthy alliance with the elite (who are difficult to please), Machiavelli shows his true political stance when he says that the prince must rely on the people, "for the objectives of the people are less immoral than those of the elite, for the latter want to oppress, and the former not to be oppressed" (32).

This thought is so important that it is also found in his *Discourses*. In chapter 5 of book 1, Machiavelli says, "And doubtless, if we consider the objectives of the nobles [or elite] and of the people, we must see that the first have a great desire to dominate, while the latter have only the wish not to be dominated, and consequently a greater desire to live in the enjoyment of freedom" (1950: 121–22; brackets added; translation slightly modified). Freedom is then the measure of an ethically grounded politics for Machiavelli. It is what motivates his writing, and it is the very realistic alternative to the system of domination that disfigures reality in the closedness and necessity of what merely is. Yet freedom is already there, present in what is as its potentiality and concrete possibility, as its flight and exit. It is, in other words, the ontological and ethical grounding of another and better world. But who desires freedom and is therefore closer to it? Machiavelli is very clear about this: the people, because they simply do *not* want to be dominated and oppressed.

Speaking of the modern prince—which cannot be a "real person" or a "concrete individual" but "an organism, a complex element of society in which a collective will . . . begins to take concrete form" (1971: 129)—Gramsci says that what is at stake, in addition to an economic reform, is also an "intellectual and moral reform" (133). He says, "In men's consciences, the Prince takes the place of divinity or the categorical imperative, and becomes the basis for a modern laicism and for a complete laicisation of all aspects of life and of all customary relationships" (ibid.). What this entails is a complete remake of the world, closer to the earth, the earthliness of thought as is clear from the following important passage from his discussion of Marxism or the philosophy of praxis. This is what Gramsci says: "The philosophy of praxis is absolute 'historicism,' the absolute secularisation and earthliness of thought, an absolute humanism of history" (465). The modern prince, then, as a new ontological, political, and ethical perspective on life, is a "myth," an earthly and poetic figure expressing the desire and struggle for freedom and happiness, pointing to the good life that must be built.

CHAPTER 2

THE ETHICAL OBLIGATION
TO DISOBEY AND RESIST

Nowhere is the distinction between ethics and the law more apparent than in the notion and practice of resistance and civil disobedience. From what we have seen in the previous chapter, it is clear that both ethics and the law *command* one to act in a certain way. For Thomas Hobbes, everything can be reduced to the law, and ethics is completely excluded from the determination of right and wrong, of just and unjust. For Schmitt, the politics of friend and enemy is the presupposition of the legal order and the state. For him, too, ethics and morality cannot play a role in political life. In a very technical (and narrow) sense, the political is autonomous from all other spheres of life. However, we saw that the construction of the figure and character of the enemy—contrary to what Schmitt believes—always has strong moral connotations. Unavoidably, the enemy becomes the evil one, who must be destroyed. Different from what Schmitt teaches, wars are regularly fought in the name of humanity, and the enemy is seen as less than human, totally dehumanized. In a sense, humanity, an ethical concept, taints the purity of Schmitt's notion of the political. However, the problem may lie precisely in the fact that humanity is excluded from the political. To correct the problem, we have to first of all abandon the friend-and-enemy logic that for Schmitt defines the political. This abandonment can only happen through the ethical—namely, the realization that any politics divorced from ethics is an instrument of oppression, enmity, war, and death. Invariably, politics becomes dysfunctional to societies and the world; it is not simply a partisan endeavor, which in itself is not a problem, but it leads to opportunism and corruption. Yet another type of politics is possible, one that is not only instrumental but also functional and organic to its communities and more broadly to the world as a whole. This type of politics has humanity—that is to say, ethics—at its center and at its margins; it is concerned with the humanity of any given situation. Its only enemy is any system that intends to oppress, humiliate, and destroy humanity—not in the abstract, but in any given concrete and singular situation. The point is not, as Schmitt seemed to fear, to wage a war in the name of humanity, but rather to exit the logic of war and build the conditions for a new political and, more important, ethical life. Humanity constitutes itself as a political subject as a way of stating that any politics deprived of ethics and defending the particular interests of a group, a caste, a class, rather than the universality and commonality proper to the human condition, is "political" only in a very equivocal sense, and it is in fact the result of measures of violence and usurpation. Although I will go back to this later, it might be important to notice here that Karl Marx's concept of the proletariat as a revolutionary class points precisely to that universal dimension. The task of the proletariat is accordingly that of dissolving all classes, including itself as a class. Its interests and concerns are not particular, but universal.[1]

In Immanuel Kant's notion of the kingdom of ends, we saw that humanity is the nonsovereign moment of freedom. Humanity is a relation to the moral law, which can be attended to or discarded. The political choice that is faced has nothing to do with who is the friend and who is the enemy but rather embracing or not embracing the practical disposition toward justice. I am not, of course, referring to the legal sense of justice, but its ethical one. In other words, ethics is the result of a political choice. A just, or ethical, world has to be built through a political choice and through political actions. In a sense, this is simple. As the principle of the kingdom of ends states, "Treat the humanity in the others as well as in yourself, not only as a means, but also always as an end in itself." It is here that Kant distinguishes between price and dignity: what has a price can be replaced, but what has a dignity is irreplaceable. The latter is what I call the *dignity of individuation*—namely, the fact that each existence should be valued and respected in virtue of its being individuated as such, and for no other reason. Kant does not rule out price or instrumentality (i.e., being treated as a means) for the simple fact that, in a completely nonutilitarian way, he recognizes that usefulness is not a problem. We can be useful to one another without ever approaching the limit beyond which there is exploitation and abuse. Indeed, this limit is set precisely by dignity and the notion of being treated as an end in itself. This may sound idealist and even merely utopian, but it is, on the contrary, very concrete (concretely utopian), and it has in fact been practiced. Examples of this practice can be found in all situations of communal life, when people try to build something new, a different mode of relating to one another, and reshape the world. One example that is close to us is the experience of the Occupy movement at its inception and through the first months of its existence in Zuccotti Park. Contrary to what mainstream media were portraying, the sense of solidarity, commonality, usefulness, and mutual aid among all was great: cooking, speaking, cleaning, reading, organizing, caring, sweeping the square, and so on were going on

constantly. Such fluidity was only broken by the pathological law, the repression that came down with unimaginable
brutality from the City of New York and the gratuitous
(and often sadistic) violence of the police.[2]

If humanity is the nonsovereign relation to the ethical, and if the ethical is different from—at times even
at odds with—the pathological law, then being human,
or ethical (or moral), may require that the pathological (or
positive) law be challenged rather than heeded, obeyed,
or complied with. This is typically what goes under the
name of civil disobedience, a practice that has an honor-
able tradition in the recent history of the United States
and other countries, but that can be traced back to ancient
times. One clear example of this would be Socrates. Later
in this chapter, I will deal with another example, close to
Socrates in time—namely, Sophocles's *Antigone*. But let
me first address a situation closer to us by looking at Martin Luther King Jr.'s "Letter from a Birmingham Jail."

The distinction between ethics and the law is a central theme in King's letter. He addresses it by saying that
"there are two types of laws: there are just laws, and there
are unjust laws" (1992: 89). He continues, "I would
agree with St. Augustine that 'An unjust law is no law at
all'" (ibid.). For him, a law is just or unjust depending
on whether it coincides with the moral law. Any law, just
or unjust, is human made; however, the moral law, with
which any human-made law may coincide or not, is "eter-
nal and natural" (ibid.). King's philosophical reference
is not Kant but St. Augustine, as we have just seen, and
then he refers to St. Thomas Aquinas. Yet the discourse
is very similar to what we have seen in the previous chapter on Kant. Interestingly, in the next passage, King uses
the word *personality*, which is also a key word in Kant's
Critique of Practical Reason. There, personality becomes
for Kant a sort of schematism whereby a coincidence can
be established between the supersensible world of reason

and of the moral law and the sensible world of experience, action, and the positive (or pathological) law. Personality is a power that connects the two worlds, "so that the person as belonging to the sensible world is subject to his own personality as belonging to the intelligible [supersensible] world" (1981: 108). King does not use the word *personality* in exactly the same sense, but he also points to a connecting power and a schematism whereby justice or injustice becomes a whole. There is also the same movement here that we have seen in Kant's description of personality. King says, "Any law that uplifts human personality is just. Any law that degrades human personality is unjust" (1992: 89). I would like to recall here the concepts of dignity and dignity of individuation. They represent the divide between uplifting and degrading and between the just and the unjust. King applies this type of thinking to the segregation laws of his time, which is the issue he is dealing with in the *Letter*, and he shows with logical and moral rigor why they are wrong. He says, "All segregation statutes are unjust because segregation distorts the soul and damages the personality. It gives the segregator a false sense of superiority and the segregated a false sense of inferiority" (ibid.). In saying this, he is speaking not only from a moral perspective but also, and perhaps more important, from a logical and ontological one (i.e., according to the logic of the real, the logic of being). He is offering a sort of *grammar* of the ethical— namely, an unequivocal way of determining the true and the false and the just and the unjust, which cannot depend on what anybody may like or dislike and on anybody's prejudice and interest, but it is rather established by the objective meaning of personality. The false sense of superiority of the segregator and the false sense of inferiority of the segregated are both pathological forms deriving from a distortion of what human personality essentially is and must be. We are dealing with very strong ethical and ontological determinations. In other words, there is no moral relativism, no ethical uncertainties as to what is right and just or wrong and unjust. The essential point is that the same thing cannot be both just and unjust. There is no logic or grammar capable of justifying and speaking sensibly of the degradation of the human personality. The fact that this degradation has been all too real throughout human history only shows the extent of the pathologies of human societies as well as the duty bestowed on reason to correct and eliminate them. It is on the basis of a well-grounded and stringent moral logic, and not simply on the basis of what is often downplayed as a merely subjective moral discourse, that King introduces the crucial choice between obedience and disobedience. One has to obey what is "morally right" and disobey what is "morally wrong." However, it is important to keep in mind, once again, that morally right and morally wrong are not subjective determinations of human passions and interests but rather objective and universal modes generated by strict rules of ontology and by the logic and grammar of life. To oppress is morally wrong; to resist oppression is morally right. The measure of the distinction is the power that Kant calls personality: a power that when it is degraded must become counterpower, and when it is crushed by brutality and violence will find itself in the region of counterviolence. It is in this sense that King could "urge" people to disobey what was wrong—something that his critics called incitement to violence. He says, "So I can urge men to disobey segregation ordinances because they are morally wrong" (ibid.).

The distinction between the just and unjust law is seen by King in terms of sovereignty. The unjust law is the sovereign law, "a code that a majority inflicts on a minority that is not binding on itself" (ibid.). In fact, as most often is the case, it is a code that a minority (even a very small group of people, or a single person for that matter) inflicts on a majority without being bound by it. This is indeed the classic notion of the sovereign represented by the king in the classical age or by the plutocracy in our days. For King, this is where a negative concept of difference is made legal—that is, difference as oppressive discrimination. The definition of the just law is remarkably close to Kant's notion of the kingdom of ends. King speaks of "sameness made legal" (ibid.). A just law is "a code that a majority compels a minority to follow, and that it is willing to follow itself" (ibid.). Sameness here means universality since the maxim of an action, or of an entire mode of relating to one another, is made universal. Sameness also points to equality, not in the sense of a flat and grey uniformity but rather in the sense in which the law should not protect the privileges of a group of people but should be rooted in reason and be concerned with everybody's equal access to the good life. What is the same in the law of sameness is humanity itself. King could have said that commonality or universality is made legal. Perhaps it would have been easier to understand that he was indeed speaking of ethics and the moral law. However, there is also something else, something that bridges the distinction between ethics and the law: the human-made law can coincide with ethics, and this makes it just. However, there is no other way by which the law can be just. This means that the history of humanity is the history of injustice, and it has been up to Martin Luther King's and our times. The law of ethics (i.e., "sameness"—in spite of the problematic use of this word and of its correspondent, "difference") is not a law that a majority imposes on a minority but rather one that does away with the distinction between a majority and a minority insofar as all stand under it by legislating on its behalf, or through it, in a nonsovereign way. In the sovereign system of unjust laws, a code is "inflicted" on some, or many, or most people; these are conditions whereby entire groups and classes of people are oppressed, exploited, humiliated, and disenfranchised. On the contrary, in the nonsovereign system of just laws, the *compulsion* of which King speaks has its origin, not in the preference, interests, and passions of any given class of people (be it a majority or a minority) but rather in the vision of (and thus the "submission" to) the commonality of human dignity and the dignity of life. Even though King says that in this latter system "a majority compels a minority," it is obvious that there is more to it than this simple and hasty mechanism. The compulsion is—I must use this word again—the *submission* to that which has no price: the small things in life, the infinitely small, love, friendship, solidarity, the human face, the eyes of the animals (including the human animal), and the palpitation of life. This is the sameness we are talking about. This is what G. W. Leibniz (1972), for instance, calls the common concept of justice as well as the experience of the place of the other as a place of ethics and love. Compulsion then does not mean force as violence but rather force as a counteracting moment in the midst of the worst type of violence—that is, resistance to the destructive powers of the sovereign and dominant paradigm. It means directing one's regard and strength toward what is to be respected. In other words, it means (higher) obedience that is due to ethics and the law of common, as well as singular, dignity. However, as we will see next when speaking of Antigone, this type of obedience (and we have to bear with the problematic nature of this term) must appear as disobedience to the human-made law that does not coincide with dignity—namely, the unjust and pathological law.

Thus King explicitly mentions civil disobedience, which is "in reality expressing the very highest respect for the law" (1992: 90), and about which he says, "[T]here is nothing new" (ibid.). He says that Socrates practiced it. However, what is important here is the way in which he deals with the accusations according to which civil disobedience actions "precipitate violence" (92). Remaining true to his approach based on love and nonviolent protest, he also shows that the origin of violence lies in the system of injustice that makes civil disobedience actions necessary. This is a very important point often overlooked about the question of violence—a question that is almost always posed in the wrong terms. As we will see when speaking about Frantz Fanon,[3] the accusation of precipitating or promoting violence cannot be made in situations of resistance and counterviolence aiming at the liberation of an oppressed group of people. Rather, it is always important to determine the original source of violence and act on it. But it is also important to understand that what is original in violence, or in any other situation, also constitutes its essence. It is, then, possible to say that the violence contained in, and expressed by, moments and movements of counterviolence is in truth only the original and systemic violence that passes through them. The violence that is present in counterviolence is not illusory, but it is *an essential reflection* of the violence that posits counterviolence. As such, counterviolence aims at the elimination of violence, as well as the elimination of oppression, exploitation, and injustice. The original violence of a system of domination is, to use Marx's description of the system of capital or of any specific and predominant mode of production in *Grundrisse*: "[A] general illumination which bathes all the other colours and modifies their particularity" (1973: 107). If counterviolence appears as violence, and indeed if there is violence in it, this is due exclusively to the modifications brought on its colors of rightful resistance and desire for peace, freedom, and happiness by the endemic vice of sovereign power—that is, its original and essential disposition to violence. This forces the subject constituting itself as a subject of resistance and freedom to confront precisely a wall of violence and a world of unimaginable brutality from which there seems to be no exit. But how can the subject and movement of counterviolence be held responsible for the violence that invests them (often concretized in the typical actions of the police)? For King, the fact that resistance may precipitate violence is not a good reason to call it off. Indeed, that would be contrary to the demands of ethics and the moral, or just, law. He says that "it is immoral to urge an individual to withdraw his efforts to gain his basic constitutional rights because the quest precipitates violence" (1992: 92). It is the pathological law that bears all responsibility for situations of violence. It must never be forgotten that those who fight for liberation from exploitation and oppression and for a better world always and necessarily reject violence. Indeed, there cannot be a better world and a just society unless violence is rejected. Yet violence, which is another name for sovereign power and the pathological law, will not reject itself. In other words, those who profit from a system of violence will never stop reinforcing it—though they often, operating ideologically, attribute its source to the very receivers of that violence who rightfully engage in acts of resistance. It is in this sense that the compulsion of sameness becomes necessary, for it is only on that basis that difference as difference (i.e., individuating difference) can flourish. This is of course not the difference that oppresses—that is, the difference that is equal to the separation and distance of sovereign power. It is rather the difference in which the same is contained; it is the contraction of the same in a singular and thus different existent or *this*. The emergence of the sameness of difference is based on the dignity of individuation; it is, in other words, the awareness of the notion and reality that effective access to the good life is a common and universal right. The resistance based on this awareness is precisely not what "precipitates violence," but it is rather what counters and ultimately eliminates it. The essential truth is, as King says, that "[o]ppressed people cannot remain oppressed forever" (93). However, given the fact that oppression does not magically dissolve and that the oppressors are willing to try all means at their disposal to maintain their power, a struggle inevitably follows. In this struggle, resistance appears as violence because it is set up and ignited by violence. In truth, the act of resistance resists violence and counters it. The inevitability of the struggle is best exemplified by Marx and Friedrich Engels's description of class antagonism at the outset of *The Communist Manifesto*. Throughout history, all struggles against oppression and domination and all struggles for liberation and dignity can be understood in the same way. In other words, if there is oppression, there must be resistance to it. This is the way expressed by King: oppression cannot last forever. This was true during the American civil rights movement, the struggle against segregation about which King writes, as it was true of all liberation struggles against colonialism and imperialism throughout the world. It is also true today when we witness the emergence of new social movements everywhere (e.g., from the Arab Spring to the Occupy movement), which despite their differences are unified by a common desire to end oppression and the degradation of life. I will go back to this below.

There is nothing "new" about civil disobedience and resistance. Insofar as there is oppression, there will be a struggle to end it. Insofar as there is institutional, systematic, and systemic violence, there will also be derivative forms of counterviolence. Indeed, the question is not whether or not to condone violence. It is certainly not this or that episode of violence (behavioral violence) that must be considered for a proper understanding of the question but its entire structural apparatus. Violence is a pathology (exemplified by the law) and an abuse of power. There is nothing redeemable about it. On the contrary, resistance (i.e., protest and disobedience) does not precipitate violence: it highlights the violence that is always already there. Indeed, movements of resistance based on a desire for freedom and dignity do not constitute themselves as violent, as that would be absolutely self-contradictory as well as self-defeating. Rather, they are often construed and constituted as such by forms of power whose very substance is violence, which can only think and act according to a logic of violence—that is, one blind to any other truth but the notion that there is an enemy and that it must be kept under surveillance and control or destroyed. Indeed, today whatever is understood as "we, the people" (i.e., the public, the various "populations" throughout the world) is seen by these forms of power (the various manifestations of sovereign power) as *the* enemy. At times, we understand this in terms of potentiality when measures of "security" are applied to us (e.g., at airports). Other times, we see this in terms of tragic actuality, as is the case in the ongoing (now drone) war on terror or the police war on selected groups of people in the global cities.

It is easy to construe all resistance to a violent regime as violent, even simply on account of "precipitating" violence. Anyone who resists is seen as an extremist in a world (i.e., the liberal world) that likes to think of itself as a realm of sweetness and balance. In truth, to be an extremist (or a radical) or to go to the roots (the *radix*) is not in itself a problem. The question is which extreme one is going to and what roots one is reconnecting with. King asks, "Will we be extremists for hate, or will we be extremists for love? Will we be extremists for the preservation of injustice, or will we be extremists for the cause of justice?" (94). There cannot be an intermediate point here. Nor is this a case of the extremes coinciding but of "real extremes" (Marx 1975: 155). Indeed, one extreme, the one that touches on hate and the preservation of injustice, is based on the logic of the enemy; the other, which has love as its ground and substance and is concerned with justice, points to the overcoming of this logic or the dismantling of the conditions whereby there must be an enemy and there must be war. This overcoming cannot be accomplished by a docile compliance with whatever the law might be saying but rather by the political effort and action that bring the law to coincide with the demands of ethics. In a very Kantian fashion, King says, "I have heard numerous religious leaders of the South call upon their worshippers to comply with a desegregation decision because it is the *law*, but I have longed to hear white ministers say, follow this decree because integration is morally *right* and the Negro is your brother" (1992: 96; emphasis in the original). The notions of integration and brotherhood call forth once again the notion of sameness. We have seen that this might be a problematic notion. Yet in this context, its meaning is clear and so is the meaning of the other two notions. What we have here is the letting go, perhaps the dissolution, of the self into the other: the realization that the self is *another*. In other words, there is no self apart from its being another self, which is equal, in its difference to all others that are, in their difference, equally equal. Thus there is no assimilation of the other into the self, and thus no forced homogeneity or no homogeneity at all. The realization that I am another is the first step toward ethical thinking. The politics that brings about this mode of awareness is a politics of the extreme—the extreme of love and justice as we have seen. This must confront and resist the blind and stubborn violence of the institutions, the mentality of the police, the ideology of the state, and the specter of the enemy, or more precisely, of the enemy thought. This is the mode of politics for which King praises the demonstrators, and beyond the events he is referring to in his letters, he praises all those who fight for a better world of justice, equality, and love. He praises them "for their sublime courage . . . in the midst of the most inhuman provocation" (99).

It can be said that the question of resistance is undertheorized. This is due to the fact that resistance is easily construed as initiating or precipitating violence. We have seen from the letter of King (one of the icons of nonviolence) that this is the result of a mistake—certainly not an innocent mistake: resistance is nonviolent in its very character. It is the (most inhuman) provocation by the system of power (which brings about resistance and enhances it) that also constitutes the structure of violence, which is then reflected on resistance itself. On March 22, 2014, a rally in Madrid against austerity and for dignity was met by incredible police brutality, broken and thwarted by police violence. We know that austerity itself is a criminal undertaking, which has caused the misery, infirmity, and death (often by suicide) of many people in these recent years throughout Europe. The rally in Madrid was called Marchas 22M de la Dignidad, where 22M stands for the day (March 22); it was a rally and a protest for dignity. The main banner read, *No al Pago de la Deuda / No Más Recortes / Fuera los Gobiernos de la Troika / Pan, Trabajo y Techo* (No Debt Repayment / No More Cuts / Governments of Troika Keep Out / Bread, Work, and Shelter). The troika, of course, is the alliance of the European Commission, the European Central Bank, and the International Monetary Fund that is destroying the present and future of people's everyday life in Europe. As the event was unfolding and the police kept threatening the demonstrators, someone speaking from a stage repeatedly reminded the police that it was a totally legal demonstration and the police were asked to leave the square immediately. The provocation of the police was apparent. Indeed, instead of leaving, they attacked and brutalized the demonstrators. This may be the latest example as of this writing of what King means in his letter when he speaks of provocation and, implicitly, of the irony (to say the least) of accusing the protesters themselves of engaging in violence or precipitating violence. Once again, it is obvious that there is no violence in resisting but rather the resistance itself is a way of

countering the violence that is already there: the violence
of the police (which does not begin when they choose
to attack but is incited by their very presence, their mere
being there) and the structural violence that calls the resistance into existence in the first place (in the case of the
Madrid rally, this violence is represented by the austerity
measures that are crippling and killing people in Europe).

   This is a very serious problem. To use, perhaps somewhat loosely, Louis Althusser's conceptual framework, we
can say that what we see at work are both the repressive
and ideological state apparatuses. The Ideological State
Apparatuses, a plurality of them—though one is usually
dominant (the Church in the Middle Ages, the School in
our contemporary times), ensure the reproduction of relations of production, "which are in the last resort relations
of exploitation" (Althusser 2014: 247). In other words,
they ensure the fact that society stays the same. The
repressive state apparatus, which is only one, "secures . . .
the political conditions for the action of the Ideological State Apparatuses" (ibid.)—that is, the reproduction
of relations of production as we have just seen. This is
done "by force (physical or otherwise)" (ibid.). We are
thus dealing with the question of the police in its narrow and broad senses—that is, including the bureaucracy,
the various branches of administration, and so on. Indeed,
we are dealing with the question of so-called security in
the streets, on campuses, in one's private home, and on the
Internet. Especially after the revelation of Edward
Snowden about the National Security Agency's system of
surveillance, we know that the repressive state apparatus
lately has been rather active in novel ways.[4] It is perhaps
possible to say that today when the ideological state apparatuses, and in particular whichever is dominant among
them, are losing their hegemonic edge, the force and presence of the repressive state apparatus must be enhanced
and multiplied. In simple words, more surveillance and

control, more police and military presence everywhere, more drones, and so on are needed with the understanding of course that this presence is never simply a show of force (in itself threatening and abusive) but an actual and effective engagement in operations of violence, brutality, and terror. This must be done in order to leave no doubt as to the seriousness of the tasks at hand. More repression must be exerted as the ideological tools weaken and fail. This is probably not what the various regimes around the world prefer, but it is their last resort when—thanks also to the means provided by the Internet—the people of the world become increasingly sophisticated and critical thinkers, the illegitimacy of the failed governments (virtually all governments around the world) becomes clearly apparent, and their authoritative stance dwindles and wanes. They must resort to "pure" violence and total repression. However, this is also the signal that a new paradigm of power might be emerging—one that is not based on repression and authoritarian rule (whether openly authoritarian, as in an established dictatorship or hidden behind the veil of so-called democratic rule) but rather one for which power is essentially about caring. That would be the creative power to do something good for everybody and for the world, to enhance the possibility of a world of social justice and concrete happiness.

At the level of the concept—and that is not an ideal level, but it is absolutely real—resistance is a political necessity and a moral obligation. I say "at the level of the concept" because in one's personal life one can choose not to engage in resistance for whatever reason. Yet this does not change the material conditions whereby to resist is precisely not up to *one*, but it is rather already inscribed in the situation at hand. Since we are now going to look at Sophocles's *Antigone*, it might be good to start by saying that this is the difference between the positions of Antigone herself and her sister, Ismene. This is how the tragedy starts:

Antigone and Ismene, who are both Oedipus's daughters and half-sisters, are talking about the terrible tragedy that involved their two brothers, Eteoclês and Polyneices. The two brothers killed one another as they were fighting each other. Creon, their uncle and new king of Thebes, decides to honor Eteoclês as a hero for fighting for the city and punish (even in death) Polyneices, the traitor and—we might say today—terrorist: "Creon / Promotes one of them and shames the other. / Eteoclês—I heard Creon covered him beneath / The earth with proper rites, as law ordains, / So he has honor down among the dead. / But Polyneices' miserable corpse— / They say Creon has proclaimed to everyone: / 'No Burial of any kind. No wailing, no public tears. / Give him to the vultures, unwept, unburied, / To be a sweet treasure for their sharp eyes and beaks'" (Sophocles 2001: lines 22–30).

The difference between Antigone and Ismene is very clear from the outset. Antigone thinks that Creon's edict is wrong and that they should go against it. She tries to persuade her sister: "If you share the work and trouble" (41). The "work and trouble" is that of helping "this hand raise the corpse . . . (*Indicating her own hand*)" (43). Ismene has already intuited that a "dangerous adventure" (42) is being proposed. Her answer to Antigone is telling: "Do you mean to bury him? Against the city's ordinance?" (44). Obviously, that is what Antigone, for whom the city's ordinance counts nothing, means. But Ismene only thinks in terms of the law, what it allows or forbids. For Antigone, the law has already lost its force and scope: there is a higher law that is more demanding than the human-made law. The higher law has its roots in material and bodily attachment, something that is of no one's choosing: "But he is mine. And yours. Like it or not, he's our brother" (45). This type of betrayal is not even conceivable for Antigone. Ismene finds the idea "horrible" (47) for the simple fact that it is against the law, against Creon's edict. Antigone replies, "He [Creon] has no right to keep me from my own" (48). To say that the king has no right is to destroy the figure of the lawmaker, the very notion of the lawmaking activity, and the legitimacy of the law itself. There is a territory that must remain beyond the human-made law, which can be approached only by trying to coincide with it, a higher or broader territory of the moral law where edicts, ordinances, and so on are empty and void. The expression "my own" means "my life"; it means what is part of me and makes me who I am, what constitutes whatever we call the self, one's subjectivity, and so on. Indeed, here we have the emergence of a new subjectivity, a new singularity of Antigone, the law-breaking and law-despising heroine of this great philosophical tragedy. As an early example of what today we call civil disobedience, Antigone, in denying the right of the king (i.e., the sovereign, to use a much later notion not applicable to that historical time), destroys the very essence of the law, the human-made law, whose essence is truly nonessential but has the characteristic of a thwarted and disfigured contingency. In other words, the human-made law takes away the can-be and not-be modality of human situations and freedom. It gives the impression that things must be in such a way when they could actually be different. Its coercive nature is a mere fabrication, as in more modern times Hobbes would show without any hypocrisy. Yet what is even more "coercive"—but this happens at the level of a materialist ethics, of the body and affects—is the law that forces us to do what is right and just. This is the law of resistance and, if need be, disobedience and revolt.

At stake is the question of freedom as well as that of becoming a subject—the type of subjectivity, the singularity, one "chooses" to be. This is what we see as Antigone and Ismene's ways diverge and as they take opposite position vis-à-vis their relation to power: Ismene chooses to conform to this power while Antigone rebels and fights against it. Ismene will try to justify her succumbing to the fear of power and the law by saying that "it's the highest wrong to chase after what's impossible" (92). In truth, she herself has already determined that what her sister is proposing is *impossible* simply because the law says so. By calling the possible impossible, Ismene renounces her own power and agency. Instead of becoming a free (and that means rebellious) agent, she subjects herself to the culture of fear brought about by the word of the king, the order of the law. She justifies her position saying that it comes from her "very nature" (78), her inability to "take arms against the city" (79). Antigone sees through her and calls her a coward: "Go on, make excuses" (80). She also explains substantively the difference between her sister's position and her own in lines that I need to quote in full: "Go on and *be* the way you choose to be. I / Will bury him. I will have a noble death / And lie with him, a dear sister with a dear brother. / Call it a crime of reverence, but I must be good to those / Who are below. I will be there longer than with you. / That's where I will lie. You, keep to your choice: / Go on insulting what the gods hold dear" (71–77). Antigone is here speaking not only to Ismene but also to us.

On the contrary, Creon is not speaking to us or to Antigone as a human being, a mourning sister, and a singularity. He speaks to the city, by means of the law, to the equalized subjects, who are in fact deprived of all subjectivity. The decision is exclusively his: "Never, while I rule, / Will a criminal be honored higher than a man of justice" (207–208). According to Creon, the man of justice is Eteoclês, who "fought for the city, and for it he died" (194). Even today, and perhaps more so than in the past, we are so quick to praise those who *sacrifice* themselves for the city, the state, the nation, and us. The superficiality, as well as the sadistic dimension, of this type of thinking usually eludes scrutiny among politicians, lawmakers, mainstream media, and the general population who are easily manipulated into accepting those ideological premises and truths. Thus Creon is an archetype of the language of the law and politics. For him, the criminal is Eteoclês's "blood brother, Polyneices by name" (198).[5] Polyneices is split into two different persons: the blood brother and the other who has soiled his name, the one who has given his name the shameful character of crime, terror, and treason: "This man will have no grave / . . . / No one in Thebes may bury him or mourn for him" (203–204). No one in Thebes mourned for Polyneices except for Antigone, but she is less than *one in Thebes.* Or perhaps she is something more than that; she is a human being and a sister, not a mere servant of the regime or a subject of the king. She will say that much later on in the tragedy when the time comes for her to realize her homelessness, which is typical of true thinking and autonomous praxis: "No city is home to me" (853). No city, no home, aiding the enemy, or siding with the criminal and terrorist—that is the lot one can expect for doing so, and as Antigone says, that is the "reward" (903) as well. Yet it is a reward for true love, true justice, and true care.

About the one whose name is Polyneices, Creon says, "He broke his exile, he came back hungry for our blood, / He wanted to burn his fatherland and family gods / Down from the top. He wanted to lead his people— / Into Slavery" (199–202). He is easily made into *the one* who has chosen to aid the enemy and *is* the enemy. Creon's rhetoric, the rhetoric of the law and politics, reminds us of what our *useless* politicians and mainstream journalists regularly do and say when it comes to *the ones* who "betray" the order of the state, the unity of the nation, the "ethics" of the community, and so on. Indeed, the word "useless" is used by Creon to describe himself at the end of the tragedy: "Please take this useless man," says he, praying (1339). The names

of Chelsea (Bradley) Manning and Edward Snowden come
to mind. Antigone, too, chooses to aid the enemy and thus
becomes the enemy. She chooses to go against the law and
bury her brother. As a matter of fact, she is obliged to do so.
Her action can only be a scandal and a crime to the eyes of
the human-made and pathological law. Yet the meaning
of this law, from the point of view of justice (i.e., the truth of
ethics), is null and void. There is no meaning whatsoever
to the words uttered by the crazed lawmaker, the king of
Thebes, because from the point of view of a singularity that
is less (or more) than one (certainly, *no one*—and this is
the case with all singularities and subjectivities that resist
plain and total subjection), language is not about order-
ing and ruling; rather, it is about "coming home forever"
(893) in the midst of violence, danger, and homelessness—
and that is true and poetic language. This coming home is
the singularity of agency, the principle of an action that is
unexpected—that is, the action of resistance, or disobedience, such as sitting down when and where you are not
supposed to sit down (as in the iconic case of Rosa Parks)
or exposing and divulging the horrors of war (as in the
extremely brave case of Manning).

As the chorus in *Antigone* points out, there is something
exceptional and *monstrous* (376) about all this. Indeed,
the city itself, the political community, is destroyed when
what prevails is the logic of the enemy. The city is no longer possible for those who shamelessly go against "the
law of the land" and the "justice of the gods" (369–370).
In fact, this is the same as renouncing the possibility of
the good life and returning to what is perhaps less than
bare life: "plagues that are hopeless" (364). This is what
we find in the chorus's first great stasimon, whose initial
lines are a philosophical gem. There we read and hear
about the power (especially of humans) to not only create but also destroy: "Many wonders, many terrors, / But
none more wonderful than the human race / Or more

dangerous" (332–334). The description that follows, of the human race, is typical: technology, work, control of nature and of other living beings, and language. However, what stands out, perhaps, is the natural capacity for politics: "[T]he character to live in cities under law" (357). All this easily turns to disaster and terror if the ethicality of the political community is lost. This is when the human being "goes wrong" (375), for the capacity for wrongdoing and injustice is there, and it is equal to the capacity for the good life. There is here no state of nature, no war of everybody against everybody, but rather the ever-present choice, not simply between two or more courses of action, but between taking and not taking *one* course of action. The human ability to live in cities under law should not be taken to mean that the human-made and pathological law has a position of predominance in the social and political order of things, for that is precisely the reason things might go wrong. Rather, this *law* is what ties the political community to the earth, "grandest of the gods" (338), for the city is always "an earth form," as Lewis Mumford says (1938: 316). The abandonment of this type of *ethos* or character (i.e., the separation of the political from the ethical and earthly) is what constitutes the preconditions for a "daring" (Sophocles 2001: 372) whereby the city is lost. Indeed, the city "shall stand high" (371) if "the law of the land" and "the justice of the gods" are respected (369–370). Law and justice here are no mere legal terms; rather, they point to the ontological and ethical ground of the political community. The land and the gods (i.e., the commonality of the earth), as well as our subjective effort to preserve and care for them, constitute the preconditions for the good life, freedom, and happiness: "But no city for him if he turns shameless out of daring" (372). In shamelessness, which is the ethical opposite of excellence, one's character is abandoned, and that is to say, one's relation to the land (the earth) and the gods.

In discussing Heraclitus's fragment "*ēthos anthrōpōi daimōn*," which is usually translated as "a man's character is his fate," Heidegger suggests that *ethos* "means abode, dwelling place"—that is, "the open region in which man dwells" (1977: 233). The word *daimon* means "the god." According to Heidegger, Heraclitus's fragment says, "Man dwells, insofar as he is man, in the nearness of god" (ibid.). Another way of understanding this, with reference to some lines in *Antigone* we have already read (Sophocles 2001: 338, 369–372), is to say that the human condition cannot escape the justice of the gods and, grandest among them (as far as humans are concerned), the earth, whose law is not of their making. The earth would then be both *ethos* (dwelling place or character) and *daimon* (god as force or tension), naming its own relation and connectedness to the universe or nature as a whole. In other words, the earth is living as is the infinite cosmos—a thought that reaches back to the beginning of various philosophical traditions throughout the world. What remains in question is the character of our position (the human position) with respect to this understanding of nature of which humanity is a part.

The city is an expression of this daimonic force. I mean the city in its original sense of *polis*, as Heidegger suggests, is "the pole, the swirl in which and around which everything turns" (1996: 81). In the context of a "poetic dialogue between Hölderlin and Sophocles," reading the first lines in *Antigone*'s first stasimon, Heidegger traces the etymology of *polis* to the verb *pélein*, which means "to emerge and come forth of its own accord, and thus to presence" in Heidegger's words (71). It also means to move and rise and to persist by changing. The Greek word for monstrous and violent is related to it. A form of the verb *pélein* is used by Sophocles at the inception of *Antigone*'s first stasimon to indicate the *surplus*—if I may put it this way—of wonders and terrors that are proper to the human race. The

nominalization of the verb *pélein* has for Heidegger the
same meaning as *fúsis* or that which arises by itself, which is
usually translated as *nature* and is, as Heidegger says, "the
word for being" (108). Obviously, these hasty remarks do
not do justice to Heidegger's evocative and profound discussion of these points, and all I can do here is refer the
reader to what is perhaps one of Heidegger's most interesting works, his discussion of Friedrich Hölderlin's "The
Ister" (Heidegger 1996). However, these few and scattered remarks allow us to call into question the habitual
way in which we look at the political and its relation to
the ethical. Perhaps what we see here is that the daimonic
force that defines the political is inextricably linked to the
human ethical disposition—namely, the way in which we
position ourselves vis-à-vis what arises of its own accord;
or, in a different terminology, is contingently caused. To
speak generically of a human disposition in this context risks
falling into a flat discourse of universality that might be mistaken and misunderstood. Indeed, it must be shown—and
I hope I can do that in the present work—that the ethical
disposition of humanity only belongs in the struggle against
domination, oppression, and exploitation. It is, then, not a
flat universality (of the liberal kind) but rather the determination of what is needed for the good life for all. In other
words, the good life (or the lack thereof) is not something
that is given; it is the result of the way in which we position ourselves at both the ethical and political levels. The
problematic aspect of the use of the word *we* is apparent,
as there may be at least two parties claiming to be speaking for it. My contention is that the true *we* of humanity
is the one that recognizes itself in any singularity, the one
whereby each *I* is fully and equally another—not the one
for which the other must be kept at a distance and under
constant surveillance, ordered about and dominated on,
used and abused, and so on. It thus becomes a question of
power, and this power can be expressed as domination and

oppression or as care, where care comports the end of a regime of oppression and domination. In a sense, this is the main difference between Creon and Antigone. Speaking to his son and Antigone's fiancé, Haemon, Creon will say, "A city belongs to its master. Isn't that the rule?" (Sophocles 2001: 738). To which Haemon replies, "Then go be ruler of a desert, all alone" (739). Possessing and dominating cannot be reconciled with "the character to live in cities under law" (357)—namely, the character of the common. Indeed, no one *owns* the city, as the *city* means any ethical and political community from the tiniest village to the planet as a whole. The point here is not that of the notion of common property, which says that the city (or the earth) belongs to all—and common property is indeed a paradoxical notion. In fact—and this was true of the relationship of the Native Americans with their surroundings—it should be emphasized that all we can speak about is a *proper use*, rather than a possession, of both what is given and what is made. The very notion that a city *belongs to* anyone is pathology, and the rule that Creon has in mind is precisely the pathological law that sets the ruler apart from the ruled. But this is the law of loneliness and sadness derived from relations of power and production that are oppressive and exploitative in the first place. From Antigone's times to ours—that is, the times of the global 1 percent set apart from the 99 percent and of the global financial and political elites separated from people's everyday lives, dominating, oppressing, and exploiting them in every respect—the struggle has been, and continues to be, a struggle for freedom and dignity articulated through resistance, disobedience, and care.

I already mentioned the notion of the pathological law or the human-made law, which may or may not be coinciding with justice. The dialogue between Antigone and Creon about the meaning of the law is the most central locus in the tragedy for an understanding of the question of resistance and disobedience. It is also useful as an introduction to Antigone's position in relation to the question of power as care.

Upon finding out that Antigone has buried her brother, Creon says, "And yet you dared to violate these laws?" (449). Antigone replies with contempt, as the laws Creon is talking about are null and void. Her words of contempt are strong, as we will see in a moment, and we know that even today this type of contempt may lead to accusations of disorderly conduct, resisting arrest, and so on. According to Creon's law, Antigone is guilty of all this. Yet her words have the power to delegitimize the unjust laws and by extension show the pathological nature of the entire system of laws on which the city is based. Antigone says, "What laws? I never heard it was Zeus / Who made the announcement. / *And it wasn't justice, either.* The gods below / Didn't lay down this law for human use. / And I never thought your announcements / Could give you—*a mere human being*— / Power to trample the gods' unfailing, / Unwritten laws" (450–457; emphasis added). This is so powerful and clear that it does not require any comment. However, I would like to point out the words I set in italics in the previous quotation. To me, it seems clear here that justice does not belong in the sphere of action of "mere" human beings. Human societies can (and should) strive toward justice; they can bring themselves to coincide with it and thus make themselves just, yet justice itself is not of their making. A tradition in ethics that goes as far back as Plato and Socrates shows that something is either just or unjust. Language and the law (but the law is language) can manipulate the idea of justice, they can call the just unjust and the unjust just, yet they will never succeed in making unjust the just and just the unjust. The confusion about these problems arises because of a more basic confusion about the difference between absolute and relative values. Saying that something is good for me is completely different from saying that it is good (in an absolute sense). Although this is problematic, in the sense that the existence and validity of absolute values may be denied altogether, it is fundamental to understand and hold on to the distinction because what otherwise often happens is that the assumption is too easily and quickly made that good for me is as good as good—and that is a very strong and very dangerous assumption to make. Many people will, however, say that the nature of the good, the just, and so on is and must remain undecidable. But how can it be so? I think it is very easy to show that if it might be "good for" X to oppress and exploit Y, the end of oppression and exploitation is not simply good for Y, but it is a universal good. It would only be good for Y if we were talking not about the end of a system of oppression and exploitation but about a mere reversal of relations of domination. Yet that would be a poor and useless discourse and a waste of thinking time and effort. It would be a flat superficiality. Thus the end of oppression and exploitation is to be held as a good in itself, a universal good. In a sense, that is the triumph of Antigone's model of justice, according to which the determination of the just and unjust cannot be left to "whatever pleases the most powerful" (Leibniz 1989: 36).

As Antigone says, "These laws weren't made now / Or yesterday. They live for all time, / And no one knows when they came into the light" (Sophocles 2001: 457–459). This is the type of universality of the moral law we have seen in Kant and King. For Antigone, breaking the human-made law is nothing in comparison to the prospect of breaking "the gods' unfailing, / Unwritten laws" (456–457). Indeed, the question is not whether one lives or dies, and the possibility of dying for the sake of uprightness is not the worst fate that might befall a human being. As Socrates says in the *Apology*, it would be wrong to

think that "a man who is any good at all should take into
account the risk of life or death; he should look to this only
in his actions, whether what he does is right or wrong,
whether he is acting like a good or a bad man" (Plato
2002: 28 b–c). Socrates continues, "It is not difficult to
avoid death . . . ; it is much more difficult to avoid wick-
edness, for it runs faster than death" (39 b). Those who
believe that by means of force and violence they can break
the spirit of resistance are wrong because the ontology of
resistance is more powerful and much more grounded than
any utilitarian calculus might be. Antigone does not concern herself with death because death is unavoidable: "I'll
die in any case, of course I will, / Whether you announce
my execution or not," Antigone says to Creon (Sophocles
2001: 461–462). Indeed, "the pain is nothing" (466),
which is instead what utilitarian thinking tries to avoid
at all costs. The ontology of resistance and the ethics of
defiance are fueled by an obligation, which is, perhaps
paradoxically, the greatest expression of freedom—that is,
to reject any given order of things for the sake of laws
that must be obeyed: "Hades longs to have these laws
obeyed" (519).

Antigone challenges the distinction between good and
bad and right and wrong, determined by the pathological,
human-made law. Perhaps in Hades things stand differently. This is to say that perhaps according to the true
concept of justice, what is legally right is in fact wrong,
and what is legally wrong is in fact right. And when Creon
remarks that an enemy remains an enemy even in death,
Antigone replies that she sides with love, not with hatred
(520–523). Accordingly, she renounces her place within
a city where the logic of the enemy rules. Her choice is
to return to the true home and be with her people. The
destruction and misery that soon overtake Thebes point
to the futility of methods of violence in running human
affairs. These methods are futile and counterproductive;

they are self-defeating ways when they try to break the ontology of resistance and the essential freedom characterizing the human condition. Yet this is something that in the course of human history has yet not been understood.

CHAPTER 3

DEACTIVATE VIOLENCE

HUMAN INSECURITY, THE ENEMY, AND THE OTHER

On December 7, 2005, Rigoberto Alpizar, a man with bipolar disorder, was shot dead at Miami International Airport by two federal air marshals. The justification for the killing was that Alpizar allegedly claimed he had a bomb. This remains controversial, as some fellow passengers on the plane with Alpizar, who was trying to leave in a state of great agitation, denied he ever uttered the word *bomb*. What is certain is that Alpizar's wife followed him as he ran off the plane, and she was shouting that he was sick, had a mental illness, and was suffering from bipolar disorder and had not taken his medication that morning. A former air marshal instructor said to NBC News that air marshals are trained to ignore potential "distractions" when confronting a threat.[1] Ultimately, it was decided that they had acted by the rules, appropriately responding to a threat. Obviously, this is not the place to debate whether the word *bomb* was uttered or whether the air marshals acted according to their training rules. What is rather important is to highlight the human cost of a completely irrational approach to the question of security, which has reached its zenith in the so-called post-9/11 era. It is also important to stress the constant danger most vulnerable individuals (e.g., people with disabilities) are facing. For them, in particular, security itself becomes the greatest threat. Because they are seen by the state and its police as the other par excellence, they become a potential or actual enemy. They are identified as a threat, but in reality, they are at the receiving end of a greater and incredibly terrifying threat. Shooting people who are ultimately harmless but who *appear as* a threat to the police has become so common that it must be addressed in a special way. Indeed, Alpizar is not an isolated case, but it is paradigmatic of a situation that repeats itself indefinitely and has become one of the greatest obstacles to real human security. Perhaps what should first be called into question is this appearance—that is to say, what makes anyone appear as a threat? The short answer is simple, yet complex at the same time: otherness. It is the other—the one who looks like a criminal, a terrorist, a vagabond, someone who is "up to no good," and so on—that calls forth a decisive response. Yet the human cost of all this remains concealed in what in the appearance itself does not appear.

Following the framework set up in Chapters 1 and 2, what I am saying here is that there is evidence that the enemy logic is at work in our societies in various ways. In this chapter, I take as a series of illustrations cases of excessive use of force by the police and the military as well as cases of outright atrocity and brutality. The idea is that the regime of the police is everywhere; in other words, the repressive state apparatus is performing an enhanced function today, perhaps due to the system's weakened hegemony at the ideological level.[2] Everybody in our society is a potential enemy for the system. Consequently, the system is everybody's enemy. However, there are three categories of people that can be said to be more at risk, regardless of whether we confine ourselves to the limits of any city or nation or whether we speak globally. They are the categories of disability, race, and foreignness. Still, they are all part of a broader category: poverty. Indeed, the state of war we are experiencing today is essentially that of a class war, as it has always been. However, this class war, according to the notion that class is not simply an economic category, is not essentially economic in character. The class against which the system is at war is the class of the other. This is the class the system fears and on which it intends to instill fear. The other is the enemy; the enemy is the other. The enemy/other is the one who looks different and lives and behaves differently, or so at least the system perceives. The three categories of disability, race, and foreignness are used for the sake of analytic clarity, but it is obvious that there is overlapping among them; in other words, the whole question is overdetermined. It is also true that different categories could be used as well. However, these three categories give rise to specific forms of institutional and social (pathological) behavior, which becomes essential to the repressive needs of the system: xenophobia, racism, and generalized discrimination against whoever is deemed to be the other. Moreover, in the eyes of the system and of the individuals who partake in the administration of its power and benefit from it, the threat inherent in their ill-conceived notion of the other suffices to maintain and promote (potential or actual) measures of violence that, they claim, society needs for the sake of security. Their notion of security becomes the measure and reason for the utter insecurity for an increasingly large number of people. Human insecurity is the result of a politics of fear and terror constantly visited on populations the system perceives as potential or actual threats. Once again, Thomas Hobbes's "sincere" analysis and judgment that political societies need a coercive power that keeps everybody in awe and terror (Hobbes was not afraid of using the word *terror* in this respect), in order to find some degree of permanence (and "peace"), has been distorted into a cynical calculus by means of which the vast majority of the world's population has been deprived of true freedom and of the capacity of having access to measures of happiness. The rhetoric behind all this is that it is done for the sake of the people themselves, those very people whose lives are crippled, disfigured, and destroyed. It is done—it is claimed—for the sake of security and the defense of society.[3]

I started this chapter with the case of Rigoberto Alpizar, a man with bipolar disorder killed by air marshals at Miami International Airport in 2005. This is only one in a long series of similar tragic cases. Although my argument will not be strengthened by adding more examples to it, I want to mention a few other cases. The first is a very recent one: the killing by the Albuquerque police of James Boyd, a homeless man with a possible schizophrenic condition, on March 16, 2014. In this case, the video taken by the police themselves went viral on the Internet, and it clearly shows what the police, in the absence of such evidence, usually have an easy time denying: their quick resort to excessive force and brutality.[4] Boyd was being arrested for camping illegally in the Albuquerque foothills when the situation escalated. In the video, he appears to be complying with police orders, yet he was shot repeatedly for no clear reason and then died in the hospital the next day. Anyone who watches the video will realize how unjustified the police action was. The next case is the beating of Gilberto Powell, a 22-year-old man with Down syndrome by a Miami-Dade police officer on September 14, 2011.[5] Powell was walking home when he was stopped by some police officers because they noticed a bulge in his waist band. The bulge turned out to be his medical colostomy bag. However, before the officers determined that, the situation escalated into a beating, which the police justified in the usual manner: disorderly conduct, resisting arrest, and so on. It might be that Powell, knowing he was innocent of all wrongdoing, got frightened by the situation and tried to flee or reacted against the police, as they claim. What remains in question is why—and this goes beyond Powell's situation—the public's fear of the police cannot be justified while the police themselves may always lay claim to any perceived threat against them. In fact, people's right to resist arrest should be part of the generally accepted notion of self-defense. In other words, if it is true that the police usually approach people they deem suspicious in a rather aggressive way, why should not these people—especially when they are aware they have done nothing wrong—perceive that as a threat? I am not asking this question from a legal point of view but from an existential one. Regretfully, cases of police brutality are far too numerous and increasingly common here in the United States and elsewhere. The very notion of the police should be rethought; the institution as we know it should be dismantled. In fact, the police should be an institution guaranteeing the proper function of the polis (the community); thus, it should organically rise from, and at all times be accountable to, the community itself. Yet, at the present stage and for the most part, the police only show a mentality of handcuffing and beating, arresting, humiliating, not listening to, and abusing people. The famous case of the arrest of the prominent African American scholar Henry Louis Gates by the Cambridge police is only a high-profile example of what goes on everywhere regularly and in a much more violent manner. Gates was arrested for disorderly conduct after becoming understandably enraged by the arrogance of the (white) police officer who followed him into his house demanding he identify himself because a neighbor had alerted the police to some suspicious activity around his house. What is striking here is the notion that even talking back to the police when you are in earnest and have done nothing wrong, yet are being abused in some ways, is itself something that will be criminalized. This, however, rests on something much more striking, a broader and more problematic notion, often acritically accepted, according to which the life of a police officer is more valuable than any other life, or worthier of respect. Philosophically, this is in fact indefensible. As we have seen speaking of Immanuel Kant's notions of the categorical imperative and the kingdom of ends, dignity cannot be measured. In most, if not all, cases of police brutality, the original breach of human dignity starts as an action by the police, who then retreat into this phantom world of perceived threats and lese majesty. They subsequently construe any understandable reaction to their original breach of dignity as an obvious criminal act, which must be handled accordingly—that is to say, handled with force. The possibility of a misunderstanding is ruled out until it becomes too late to step back from situations of unnecessary and regretful violence. We often speak of the use of excessive force, but force can always be said to be excessive if we look at it, for instances, from a Taoist point of view—namely, the point of view according to which all action has to be effortless or nonaction. This is not simply a beautiful but unpractical thought. Rather, it reaches into the very essence of dignity and the respect for dignity and autonomy. In fact, dignity and autonomy are completely taken away in encounters with force, let alone by the exertion of excessive force. The return from this state of affairs requires some essential and true (critical) thinking, which is necessarily absent when force is the first and main resort. The enemy logic is what determines the deplorable state of affairs whereby anybody's life remains in constant danger, not because of the war of everybody against everybody as in Hobbes but because of the now open, now hidden state of violence that the system itself unleashes against society and the war that it wages on everyday life.

There are those who are closer to the danger. We have already seen some examples, and we will see more from others. They are those against whom the system most aggressively unleashes its crippling and lethal power. They are also most often the weakest and neediest, against whom at times the generic nature of violence inherent in the present system takes on an especially vicious and sadistic dimension. Such was the case of the brutal and fatal beating of Kelly Thomas, a homeless man who had schizophrenia and who was gratuitously and viciously murdered by police officers in Fullerton, California.[6] As in other similar cases, we have a video footage, without which the whole tragic event would be unknown, buried in state bureaucracy, and passed off as business as usual. The video, however, shows a big police officer deliberately provoking and starting beating the skinny and confused Thomas in a desolate place near a bus station and bus depot in Fullerton. Other officers are present and join in the violence. One repeatedly hears the poor young man asking for help, begging the officers to stop. The photos of his smashed, disfigured face reveal the monstrosity of a system that calls itself just, fair, rational, democratic, and so on. Here, once again, we have not an isolated but a paradigmatic case of the repressive state apparatus exercising its might against the frailest expressions of life.

Failing to recognize that *anyone* is another, and thus there is no other, hypostatizes the concept of the other as such, which is seen according to a pathological view of difference. Thus the one that does not recognize itself as being another and refuses to see itself as different attributes otherness and difference to all singularities that do not conform to, or comply with, its own usurpation of sameness and identity. But how can this one do so? It can on the basis of an appropriation of forms of power or the establishing of power relations that essentially exclude many or most singularities from having access to the "enjoyment" of freedom. These singularities are kept in a state of necessity where control, surveillance, discipline, punishment, debt, and so on play the most important function.

The slightest deviation from the position and sense of direction assigned by the system to each singularity is seen by the system itself (the *one* as such, the sovereign) as defiant, offensive, and punishable. Singularities are obviously not even acknowledged as such (i.e., *as singularities*); they make up the crowd, the mob, the masses, or the "confusion of a disunited multitude" (Hobbes 1994: 111). Under control, as in the peculiar slogan "United we stand," they form the people, the nation, and the like. Uncontrolled, they fragment and dissolve into the Hobbesian "confusion."

Anyone seemingly "out of place" and/or "up to no good" has to be at least *interpellated*. To be sure, one already is, or has been, interpellated in the determination of its being precisely out of place and/or up to no good. Now the question is that of identification, interrogation, and everything that follows from stop-and-frisk practice[7] to torture and death. In other words, the singularity thus interpellated, bathed in the colors of otherness and difference, must respond and clear itself of all possible misunderstanding and all potential accusations of wrongdoing. However, it must do so by way of showing submission and humility. Any spontaneous expression of itself as a singularity will count as defiant and offensive; any reaction to the original violence encountered in the very process of being stopped and questioned, stopped and frisked, arrested, beaten, tortured, and so on is to be taken as a sign that, yes, there were reasons for finding that singularity suspect or the so-called reasonable grounds for suspicion, a logic highly behavioristic in nature. Even when there is none, the danger of a threat is easily fabricated: a state of exception is brought forth, which will justify all unimaginable violence to follow. To illustrate these points, I will focus on the case of Trayvon Martin, the 17-year-old Florida teenager killed by a self-styled neighborhood watchman in 2012; the stand-your-ground law (an example of the abuse of the notion of self-defense); and the stop-and-frisk law in New York. I will draw a formal as well as concrete analogy between these phenomena in the United States and the global realities of the so-called war on terror, especially with reference to the increasingly common drone strikes that are leaving a trail of blood across the globe.

Martin's beautiful face has sadly become emblematic of a widespread regime of racist violence grounded in police mentality that is becoming increasingly entrenched in American everyday life while sharing elements of a broader attack on people's security everywhere. Looking at a photo of Martin, no one would think of the idea of the enemy. Yet George Zimmerman, the man who killed Martin, saw him as the enemy on that rainy evening in Sanford, Florida. Martin was not from Sanford but was visiting with his father. On the evening of February 26, 2012, he was walking around, having gone to a convenience store to buy something, when Zimmerman spotted and followed him. His face, his demeanor, his hoodie seemed to Zimmerman clear enough reasons for suspicion. Martin seemed to be "up to no good," Zimmerman said.[8] There was a confrontation, and soon, Martin was dead, shot by the self-styled security guy. Although the stand-your-ground law was not used during the trial that unbelievably found Zimmerman not guilty, the principle and spirit of his defense had much to do with the use and abuse of the notion of self-defense. The whole country was galvanized. Even Barack Obama, who is forgetful of his own role as a global vigilante, weighed in on the situation, saying that if he had a son, "he would look like Trayvon."

Although Zimmerman was not a police officer, his mind-set reflected the logic of the police (if we can speak of logic here): supremacist, racist, and thoughtless. This is not necessarily the way in which an individual police officer will think and act. I have met police officers as students in my classes who have a very sophisticated and critical outlook. However, the logic of the police, which is the same as the enemy logic, goes beyond what any single individual may want or be able to do, and it is a necessary feature of the repressive state apparatus. For instance, the controversial stop-and-frisk law in New York has little to do with the initiative of individual officers. Some of them strongly oppose it. Yet it has become a structural measure for the control of the city's population and, as such, an extremely useful instrument in the hands of the city's political and financial elites. The stop-and-frisk law is predicated on the same mentality that made Zimmerman act the way he did: become suspicious of Martin, follow and confront him, and finally kill him. The stop-and-frisk law has been justified by people like former New York City mayor Michael Bloomberg (who once called the New York Police Department [NYPD] his own private army)[9] and former New York City police commissioner Raymond Kelly.[10] Essentially, their justification for this racist law (in the opinion of many) has to do with the issue of security. But it is precisely in situations like this that we realize how problematic it is to speak thoughtlessly about security. The question is, security for whom? In fact, what is called security (for some) always implies utter insecurity for many people. In the case of the stop-and-frisk law, as has been documented, young black and Latino men especially live in a constant state of insecurity. Not only can they be repeatedly stopped and frisked at any time for being in the "wrong" part of town or looking as if they are "up to no good" (just as Zimmerman said of Martin), but any instance in which they are stopped and frisked by the police can easily escalate into a tragic event, because fundamentally, the police do not think; they are trained not to. See, for instance, the case of Alvin, a young Harlem

teenager who was able to record one of his many encounters with the police. In the recording, when he asks the
police why they are constantly stopping him, they reply
that he is stopped "for being a f——g mutt."[11] In one
of the most recent cases of police brutality in New York
City, which took the life of Kimani Gray, a young African
American man from East Flatbush, Brooklyn, the tactics
described are typical of the stop-and-frisk policy, which
at times precisely creates the conditions for tragic results.
One more relatively recent tragic case was the killing of
Ramarley Graham, an 18-year-old African American man,
who was not stopped and frisked on the street but was
followed into his own house by members of the NYPD
Narcotics Enforcement Unit and shot dead in his bath-
room on the basis of the usual pretext that, just like in
the case of Gray, Graham had a weapon in his hands.[12]
In both cases, neither a gun nor any other weapon was
found. Around the time of the killing of Gray, some police
officers took the stand to denounce and expose the racist
law, notably officers Adhyl Polanco and Pedro Serrano.[13]

This violence is not limited to the streets when supported
by a law, such as the stop and frisk. It is more widespread
and ominous to the point that on occasion it takes on the
form of something similar to a night raid. Such was the
horrifying case of Kenneth Chamberlain Sr., who was killed
by police officers in his home in White Plains, New York.[14]
Chamberlain, a 68-year-old marine veteran and former
correction officer who had a heart condition, was in his
home early in the morning of November 19, 2011, when
the police arrived after being alerted by a medical emergency call. Chamberlain's LifeAid medical alert device had
accidentally gone off, so the company had placed the call.
Chamberlain asked the police to leave, saying he was fine.
However, they insisted on seeing him. But because he
would not open the door, they broke it down, tased him,
and finally killed him. The horrific sequence of events,

caught on video camera and audio tape, saw a crescendo of insults and racial slurs, and finally, the worst physical and lethal violence.[15] The White Plains police department did not release the names of the officers involved in the assault and killing of Chamberlain, and it took the courage of *New York Daily News* journalist and *Democracy Now!* cohost Juan González to have those names discovered and made public.[16] It seems that in cases like this, the stand-your-ground principle (or the Castle doctrine that predates it) no longer counts. Usually, if a situation of this kind continues for some time, it is framed as one in which someone has "barricaded" himself and is thus resisting arrest and obstructing the work of the police. What is then returned to the law and the police is the sovereign power to do as they please with individual lives—that is, singularities that are disrespected and crushed by the system. To put an end to this state of affairs, which is the norm throughout the world, we need a rethinking of the concept of the law out of the separateness of sovereignty and a total dismantling and reforming of the institution we know as the police, whose repressive function must stop. A safeguarding institution should have a function of care; it should engage power as care. Needless to say, this entails the overthrow and elimination of the present regime of violence, the concrete material and cultural shift to the not-yet of ethics, dignity, and freedom.

Using perhaps the simplistic and problematic distinction between the local and the global, we can say that the police brutality that happens at the local level is structurally analogous to the actions of the global police. Both, of course, happen locally insofar as their victims are always specifically situated. However, by global police I mean the military (especially US military) and the various paramilitary formations, the contractors (e.g., Academi [previously, Blackwater]), and so on. What I particularly want to call attention to is the current drone war that is mainly going on in countries like Yemen, Afghanistan, and areas in Pakistan (in particular, Waziristan). This war extends to Somalia, in the Horn of Africa.[17] It is a very big area of the world (and very explosive at that) that is being policed today from above and afar. Drones are unmanned aircrafts piloted from before a computer screen thousands of miles away from their sphere of action and destruction. I will go back later to an analysis of the US attempt at justifying the use of drones.[18] For now, I only want to draw a parallel between the violence we have seen in some US towns and cities and the violence experienced by various people throughout the world because of drone strikes.

The most striking parallel is certainly between the killing of Martin in Florida and of Abdulrahman al-Awlaki in Yemen. Both of them are American teenagers who had done nothing wrong but became the victims of a similar paradigm of violence based on the obsessive logic of security. The racist mentality embodied by Zimmerman, according to which a black teenager must be up to no good if he is walking around a neighborhood in which he does not belong (with a hoodie on, etc.), is the same as the racist mentality according to which any man of military age in Yemen, Waziristan, and so on, is also up to no good and indeed potentially a terrorist. In the case of al-Awlaki, it is not entirely clear why he was killed, as the White House and State Department have refused to answer any question. Robert Gibbs, a former White House spokesperson, has incoherently suggested that "[y]ou should have a far more responsible father if they are truly concerned about the well being of their children."[19] Obama never said—as he had done in the case of Trayvon Martin—that his hypothetical son might also look a little like Abdulrahman al-Awlaki. Al-Awlaki was the son of Anwar al-Awlaki, a Muslim cleric and an American citizen with possible ties to al-Qaeda who was in fact extrajudicially killed in Yemen by a US drone strike on

September 30, 2011, two weeks before the same thing happened to his son. The difference between the two events
is that we have a targeted drone assassination in the case
of Anwar al-Awlaki, whereas in the case of his 16-year-old
son, Abdulrahman al-Awlaki, the type of strike probably
was what is usually referred to as a *signature* strike. The
difference between the two types of extrajudicial and thus
illegal killing is that the former, as its name clearly says,
is one in which someone is sought out and targeted for
an assassination based on possibly true but not judicially
established accusations of terrorist activity. This strike is
determined by Obama's infamous (Terror Tuesday) secret
"kill list."[20] The second type, possibly the most common,
is one in which anybody who appears as potentially engaging in broadly construed terrorist activities—for example,
a group of men (though often that also includes women
and children) gathering together or walking in the moun-
tainous paths of, say, Waziristan—can be blown to pieces
and pulverized with the holy and bloody signature of
democracy and freedom.[21]

Both Martin and al-Awlaki are expressions of the representation of the enemy, punished and eliminated not for
what they had done (for they had done nothing wrong)
but for what they were and, according to the pathology of
that representation, what they could one day do. In the
case of al-Awlaki, this is what Jeremy Scahill also says in
Dirty Wars: "Like a tale from Greek mythology, Abdulrahman was killed not for what he'd done, but for who
he might one day become."[22] The analogy is not limited
to the cases of Martin and al-Awlaki, but it is broader and
it indicates that the same police mentality and logic of
violence links the global and the local. On the basis
of our determination of sameness (who we are) and of
our established norm, otherness must be contained, controlled, repressed, disciplined, and punished. The other
is the enemy, always potentially threatening. Preemptive

measures become necessary so that one acts not simply on the actuality of the threat, but on its potentiality.
However, even this would be a charitable way of looking
at the atrocious and tragic reality of these situations. In
truth, in most if not all cases of police and military brutality, the threat is neither actual nor potential. The threat,
thus the imminence of a threat or state of emergency, is
entirely fabricated. This is obvious in the two cases I am
currently using as tragic illustrations of this state of affair,
the cases of Martin and al-Awlaki. However, all other cases
of police brutality I referred to previously and all other
cases of innocent people dying in drone strikes (especially
of the signature type)—in other words, all collateral damage in this insane war against what is dearest and frailest in
life—point to the same essential truth: there is no threat
other than what the system itself fabricates, and there is no
enemy other than the system itself.[23] The case of Mamana
Bibi, the Pakistani grandmother who was blown to pieces
by a missile in a drone strike as she was picking okra with
her grandchildren, is still another tragic example of that.[24]
So are the many people who die in drone strikes as they
attend a wedding or other similar events.[25] The usual justification is that in the just and heroic search for the enemy,
there is unavoidable collateral damage; in the attempt at
bringing about a state of security in cities and in the world,
humanity gets in the crossfire. Yet the rhetoric continues
that there is little to be done about this, for all happens
for the sake of the security of a city, a nation, the world,
and thus of humanity itself. Obviously, there has never
been a greater falsity in political discourse. Carl Schmitt
is right when he says that the very notion of humanity is
thus usurped.[26] He is wrong in leaving humanity out of
the political and in the sphere of ethics alone, for politics
has this great ability to misappropriate and abuse ethics
itself. Instead, what humanity has to do is constitute itself
as a political subject with universal aspirations and a radical

program. The singularity that humanity is—as evident by its contraction in each concrete human being—has to dismantle and destroy the present structure of power as violence, eliminate the conditions for its reproduction by taking a turn toward what is truly meaningful in individual and collective life. This cannot be the stubborn accumulation of wealth and the rise to ever-higher levels of dominance. All historical wisdom teaches us that this accumulation of wealth and this insanity about domination are not at all what the good life promises and might indeed be. Rather, the good life consists of understanding; loving and being loved; caring for oneself, the others, and the world; and creating the conditions whereby life can flourish rather than being buried in rubble, disfigured by poverty, and threatened by constant insecurity at all levels. In short, *staying human* is the task.[27]

There are some necessary preconditions for this change to happen. They entail a destructive and a constructive mode. Many institutions must be abolished: the police, the military, the prison, and the state.[28] There should be no more weapons and borders: this seems to be a reasonable way to move forward in the constitution of a radically different world. Education and care must replace the unthinking mechanism of the law as violence, where the law only expresses its lawless and unethical origin and foundation. The method to bring about this radical change is not the war that ends all wars, as feared by Schmitt. Rather it is the end of the war mentality and of war itself.

To the potential objection that what I suggest earlier (i.e., the abolition of the repressive state apparatus and so on) is simply impossible, I answer that this claim to impossibility is precisely Ismene's position when her sister, Antigone, challenges her (see Chapter 2). Very often, we call something impossible; in truth, it is in the realm of contingency and is thus possible. As John Duns Scotus following Avicenna says, "Those who deny that some being is contingent should be exposed to torments until they concede that it is possible for them not to be tormented" (1987: 9). In light of the current situation of widespread (local and global) institutional violence—which sees the complicity of politics, the law, and the police—it is imperative to formulate a discourse that shows this contingency and highlights the lack of legitimacy of these forms of power. Indeed, discourse (language and the word) is what constituted power fears most. In some areas of the world, dissent and speaking the truth to power are dealt with in the most Draconian ways. However, the difference between a country like Egypt, where recently over one thousand people have been sentenced to death (529 of them accused of the murder of a single police officer during the unrest around the time of the fall of Mohamed Morsi), and a country like the United States, where people are jailed for political and nonpolitical reasons and put to death in many of the states in often highly controversial cases, is only one of degree, not kind. To illustrate this point, I want to briefly mention the very recent case of Cecily McMillan, an Occupy protester found guilty of assaulting a police officer.

As I write, the breaking news of McMillan's conviction in New York City causes dismay to many people. Accused of assaulting a police officer during the celebration of the first six months of the Occupy Wall Street movement, McMillan found herself in jail at Rikers Island awaiting her sentence, which came on May 19, 2014. She was sentenced to 90 days in prison, and actually served nearly two months, being freed on July 2.[29] Apparently, on the night of the incident, she elbowed an NYPD officer as she instinctively reacted to the officer grabbing and bruising her right breast. She was subsequently beaten up, taken to the hospital, and later arrested.[30] Her elbowing a police officer counts as an instance of assault, while the original assault on her by the police officer is brushed away by the law. This is a tragic example of the paradigm of violence I have been pointing out. It repeats the prejudice according to which the life and security of a police officer have a higher value than the life and security of anyone else. In truth, life and security should have equal value for all human beings: there is no more or less, better or worse, and superior or inferior. Yet, if anything, an assault by the police on any member of the community should count as a greater crime than when the police themselves are allegedly assaulted, for they have a greater power and thus a greater responsibility. The usual claim that they feared for their safety is inadmissible because the nature of their job is such that concern about their safety should be the last, not the first thought—just like a captain of a sinking ship will not first be concerned about his safety. To avoid any misunderstanding, I am not defending or justifying any type of assault or violence. What I am saying is something very different, which is usually left unsaid. I am saying that in all cases of police (or military) brutality, we hear the same type of rhetoric justifying their actions. It is an a priori justification, which rests on the prejudice I mentioned earlier, against which the public, the community, is helpless. This gives the police (or the military) a degree of impunity that greatly hurts individuals, communities, societies, and the world. My contention is that anyone entrusted with security and public safety should be more engaged than others in the maintenance of orderly and ethical conduct, not by way of imposing it on others but by imposing it first of all on themselves. The argument often made is that they need a greater degree of freedom because they put their lives on the line. However, this is a poor argument. Everybody's life is constantly in danger, and in any case this cannot become an excuse for forceful and violent behavior—and for a culture of impunity.

To go back to the case of McMillan, the political message is clear: there will be a crackdown on all forms of dissent, and the constituted order (the alliance of financial capital and political maneuver, of the criminal justice system and the police) will not allow any criticism. We live in a police state that does not even try to conceal the fact that the gun is its law and violence its approach and mode of handling things. Even peaceful protest is a crime. What follows is Chris Hedges's recent account of this kind of violence:

> I watched New York City police during the Occupy protests yank people from sidewalks into the streets, where they would be arrested. I saw police routinely shove protesters and beat them with batons. I saw activists slammed against police cars. I saw groups of protesters suddenly herded like sheep to be confined within police barricades. I saw, and was caught up in, mass arrests in which those around me were handcuffed and then thrown violently onto the sidewalk. The police often blasted pepper spray into faces from inches away, temporarily blinding the victims. This violence, carried out against nonviolent protesters, came amid draconian city ordinances that effectively outlawed protest and banned demonstrators from public spaces. It was buttressed by heavy police infiltration and surveillance of the movement. When the press or activists attempted to document the abuse by police they often were assaulted or otherwise blocked from taking photographs or videos. The message the state delivered is clear: *Do not dissent.* And the McMillan trial is part of the process.[31]

McMillan's trial was thus a show trial, aiming at sending a message to a whole population already kept in awe and terrorized by a coercive power. Whoever stands up to this power, or falls within the cracks of its own incapacity and fear, is construed as the enemy to be dealt with and eliminated. In truth, this power is the only source of violence, which must be deactivated. Its presence is what keeps the world from going forward and attaining true security, happiness and peace. It disfigures the human face, cripples life, and destroys the planet. This power must then be abolished for the sake of humanity, for *staying human*[32] is the only valuable project—a political and ethical project.

On May 7, 2014, we hear the news that a Texas police officer has killed a 93-year-old woman.[33] According to news reports, the police are "not ready" to say whether she was armed. A neighbor interviewed at the scene has rightly pointed out the absurdity of this, for even if she was armed, shooting in the air would have been enough to scare her off, and she would have dropped her gun, if she had had one. She was an African American woman; poor; and of an age at which, even if there still is health, frailty cannot *not* be there—an age where the ability to do anything is obviously diminished. It is no exaggeration to say that *this* humanity is seen by the system as the enemy to be controlled or destroyed. It is this same humanity that must become a political project, whose aim must be the deactivation of this system of violence and the ethical grounding of a new type of the political—a project in ontology.

Chapter 4

Labor, Poverty, and Migration

Sovereign Terror and
the War against Humanity

In the previous chapter, I claimed that language or discourse is what power fears most. Of course, language also means thinking, and discourse means theory. In an important and famous passage of the introduction to the critique of G. W. F. Hegel's philosophy of right, Karl Marx says, "The weapon of criticism obviously cannot replace the criticism of weapons. Material force must be overthrown by material force. But theory also becomes a material force once it has gripped the masses" (1994a: 34). Not only is theory a material force, but it is also the only force available to radical thinking that is superior to the force of the state and the system as a whole. This is so because true theory is based on ethics, which is the truth of justice and the truth in general. It does not serve the particularistic interests of a group of people, a class, or a caste, but it has universal outlook and scope. The distinction between the true and the false hinges on it. As an example, we can think about the truth that the poverty of labor is nothing but the result of exploitation and the exclusion from the wealth it produces. This truth is incontrovertible. Thus theory also shows that it is false to say that wealth rightfully belongs to those who have a legal claim to it, for the word *rightfully* would here only have a legal connotation and thus the statement would be a flat tautology. It is like saying that the slave rightfully belongs to the slave owner, which is only true within the context of a legal system that sanctions the crime against humanity that today we know slavery is. But slavery was always the same crime, even when sanctioned by the law. So we have to be careful with the use of such ambiguous words as *right* and *wrong*. In fact, when understood ethically, the word *rightfully* becomes inapplicable in a context such as this. We have already seen that the law is nothing but violence institutionalized. Thus a legal claim, for instance, of a multinational corporation to the ownership of land, water, and so on, is only based on the gun, on violence, or the threat thereof. From a radical (i.e., human) point of view, this claim is in fact false; it is null and void. But of course it is possible to get away with anything through the sheer use of material force, of violence, as the system regularly does.

"To be radical," says Marx, "is to grasp things by the root. But for man the root is man himself" (ibid.). The notion of humanity is thus central to our discourse. It is certainly not a question of political and civil rights or of the law. It is rather the question of the unity of the material conditions that make a certain legal and political order possible. I am not hinting at the base-superstructure framework, at least not in a problematic or thematic manner. I take it as a given that there is a totality of relations whereby we have a certain configuration of society—one configuration rather than another. What I am interested in highlighting here is the human import of the lack of this radicalism. Criticizing Bruno Bauer in *On the Jewish Question*, Marx points out the distinction between political emancipation and universal human emancipation (1994: 5–7). Today, going beyond the problem of religious identity, we can broaden this type of critique to include all categories of identity (race, gender, sex, nation, ethnicity, etc.). All political rights can be recognized by the so-called democratic state (i.e., the liberal state). Recognition is not a problem, as political emancipation can take place. But the real problem is the state itself and its sovereign law. This is what blocks universal human emancipation and inhibits radical theory and discourse. As Marx says, "political emancipation is not the complete and consistent form of *human* emancipation . . . The limits of political emancipation are seen at once in the fact that the *state* can free itself from a limitation without man *actually* being free from it, in the fact that a state can be a *free state* without men becoming *free men*" (7; emphasis in the original).

I have previously said that humanity has to become a political subject—that is, a political project. This is not a way of reducing human emancipation to political emancipation but rather of breaking free of the constraints of the state (even the *free* state). It is a way of working toward the dissolution of the state. It is not, then, the libertarian idea according to which anything goes, anybody is free to do as they please—provided that the *free* state remains as a guarantor. If the state is a closed system of inclusion and exclusion, whose sovereignty and identity are defined by well-marked and protected borders, humanity is the constantly infinitizing moment breaking all borders, calling into question all law, claiming the open and common. Contrary to an apparent similarity with the movement of capital, which breaks all barriers and becomes global, the infinitizing process of an ethical and political humanity does not take place by creating new enclosures but rather by liberating those already existing and producing ever-new and open forms of life and being and by standing up and out in the open (i.e., becoming the open). The state, whether *free* or *unfree*, liberal or totalitarian, must fall. Indeed, as I noted in one example earlier, the difference between the two types of states is one of degree, not kind. Consider the war of words between the United States and North Korea. The former accuses the latter of all sorts of human rights abuses; the latter correctly responds in the same way. It is obviously easy to decry abuse of power and criminalization of everyday life in a country like North Korea. We hear about the eccentric and insane Kim Jong-un, who has people executed at will, including his own uncle, and it is easy to be persuaded that something ominous is going on there. However, the real question has nothing to do with any ruler's eccentricity or insanity. Speaking of capital punishment, the free and democratic United States, where the essence of Western civilization has supposedly migrated and flourished, has seen 1,379 executions since 1976, with twenty already having taken place in 2014.[1] In the latest of these cases, the so-called botched execution of Clayton Lockett in Oklahoma on April 29, 2014,[2] was not an execution but an exhibition of the savagery and inefficiency of a state bureaucracy (which in these contexts always brings together the three institutions of law, medicine, and religion) against an individual. Lockett was to be executed by lethal injection, but he died of heart failure 43 minutes after being injected with untested drugs and 30 minutes after the execution itself had been suspended.

The point is that the *free* state does not liberate humanity, but humanity has to free itself from the state. The war against humanity does not require that humanity enter that same logic of war and fight against the system that tries to crush it. Not only is this system militarily more powerful, but it also has the cynical and criminal will to fight to the end. Thus the alternative is a method of refusal and resistance, as well as of the *rightful* reappropriation of what has been taken away, which is not only wealth in a crude economic sense but also time, space, and life—that is, true wealth. It is in this sense that the Occupy Wall Street movement remains a fundamental moment in the current process of universal human emancipation, for it

has shown that the resistance against the violence of financial capital, the state, and the system in general is alive and,
with time, able to bring about radical changes. One thing
is certain: the hour of the old regime has come. There is
no longer any true hegemonic power (if by hegemony one
also understands the capacity to persuade and convince)
but only a brute repressive force, the power of the gun and
drone. The movement may follow a subterranean route
at times, yet the system's lack of legitimacy and structure
of violence cannot even fathom the power inherent in the
human determination to deactivate violence and build
the conditions for the good life for all. This is the singular
event we are not waiting for but grounding through an
infinite number of processes aiming at reconstituting the
world—a just world.[3] This is the revolution today. Once
again, it is not a war that ends all wars but no war—a
rejection of the entire logic of war, though of course not
of resistance.

What is resistance? It is first and foremost the denun-
ciation of violence and the attempt at deactivating and
stopping it. When resistance itself appears to be violent,
it is only because the original and primordial violence is
reflected on it. In itself, resistance to violence (i.e., counterviolence) cannot be violent. That would be contrary to
its concept or the structure of its singularity. Resistance
aims at the constitution of a better world, it represents
an essential difference from the modality of violence, and
thus it has rejected violence at its very inception. However,
the violence of the system of oppression is so powerful
that it bathes all the rest in its nefarious colors. After all,
the history of the modern world (just to confine ourselves
within its limits) is a history of violence. It is the history of
sovereignties, and that is, the history of conquest, enslavement, genocide, and so on. It really makes no sense to cry
out and denounce violence as soon as an ATM machine
is smashed during a demonstration, a police car set on

fire, and so on. This is a way of trivializing and confusing the issue. First of all, most often these occurrences are very likely the doing of the system itself, the state, and the police, through their agents and infiltrators. But even when and if this is not the case, violence still remains, directly or indirectly, an instance (perhaps a consequence) of their doing. We can, then, not worry about the question whether resistance should be peaceful and nonviolent. The question is wrongly posed. From its inception, resistance moves away from the logic of war and tries to exit or deactivate the regime of violence. This is indeed the reason there is resistance in the first place. So the question that should rather be asked is, why does the system have this unquenchable need for violence? In other words, why does the system force people (and this *forcing* is already an instance of violence) to take a stand and resist? If you think of it, if instead of a regime of war and violence we had a situation of peaceful coexistence, mutual aid and solidarity, care, friendship, dignity, and love, there would be many other meaningful and creative activities to engage in rather than be dragged in a senseless standoff with a system of power protected and defended by iniquitous laws and heavily armed people (its military and police). This should be the argumentative proof that violence does not arise with and because of resistance but rather that resistance itself arises because of the violence that is already there. It is always puzzling to witness the lack of historical memory and analytic ability in our societies—where any instance of violence is taken to be as the origin rather than the result of a process of violence.

Often resistance is weakened by the lack of effective organizing. Although forms of resistance happen continuously and at all levels of everyday life, at times they remain invisible. Stanley Aronowitz has lately stressed the paramount importance of the question of organization and the need for "a strong organization" with "a vision and a strategy for change" (2014: 29).[4] However, in recent years, the internationalization or globalization of the struggle against violent power everywhere points to the possibility of new and perhaps more effective modalities of resistance. From the Arab Spring to Occupy Wall Street, the tendency seems to have been that of an instance of resistance occurring in a specific place and soon widening its scope in an impressive manner. The Arab Spring (which started in Tunisia) and Occupy Wall Street (which started in New York) have become irrefutably paradigmatic of the revolutionary *desire* (if nothing else) characterizing our present time in all parts of the world despite all their unavoidable contradictions and difficulties. Obviously, the repression against these movements has been, and continues to be, brutal. Yet they have set the stage for the type of resistance against systemic violence (at the economic and political level) that will continue to grow. Indeed, a movement or a global network of movements of humanity against violence and war is the last hope in our times of despair and terror, exploitation, and destitution. It is in this sense that I have repeatedly spoken of the need for a new political subject and suggested that this subject be humanity itself.

At times, an instance of resistance and defiance becomes tragically visible. This is how what we know as the Arab Spring started. At the end of 2010, the self-immolation of Mohamed Bouazizi, a Tunisian street vendor, started a revolutionary process that quickly brought about the fall of Zine El Abidine Ben Ali, who had been the president of Tunisia for 22 years. Bouazizi set himself on fire on December 17, 2010, and he later died of his wounds on January 4, 2011. Bouazizi's sacrifice was the ultimate act of resistance and defiance of a young man who had reached the bottom of hopelessness and despair in a situation of police brutality and state violence. Burdened with debt, Bouazizi tried all he could to support himself and his family. The police had often harassed him on the basis that he did not have a permit to sell on the streets. Then on December 17, 2010, they confiscated his merchandise, mistreated, and humiliated him once again. They had destroyed his dignity, his humanity, and Mohamed reacted in the tragic way we know.

Bouazizi has become a symbol, but he was an actual human being, whose humanity was crushed by the state and its police. Often, people point to the corruption of a state like Tunisia, the Mafioso-like conduct of its police. However, what determined Bouazizi's situation and his tragic end was not simply the local and corrupt police force and the equally corrupt government of Ben Ali but also the global and neoliberal forces of capital creating unlivable conditions for the vast majority of people everywhere. Debt, unemployment, and poverty are material instruments of violence equal to the brutality of the police or the agony and misery of war. They all participate in the constitution of a global political order that maintains itself in power by exploiting, marginalizing, oppressing, humiliating, and crippling people's lives—indeed by killing and exterminating people. Few are those who make a real profit from this: the 1 percent, as the Occupy movement says. Those who are enticed and co-opted by the system also make a miserable profit: the guards (police, military, bureaucracy, etc.). The methods used by those who are in power and profit from it are similar to those of the Mafia or the way of gangsters and thugs.[5] Obviously, they do not like to think of themselves, or be thought by others, in those terms. They will try anything to convince and persuade, use their rotten ideology in the most hypocritical way, and speak of humanitarianism and the love of life. At the same time, they control and punish, terrorize and kill, destroy the planet, and bring about misery everywhere.

Bouazizi was a worker, but he was destitute. He was a worker, but didn't have a job. He was unemployed. He worked anyway in the so-called informal sphere of the economy. He was brought to the point that he could not even do that. Many young men from Tunisia, other countries in North Africa, and those in sub-Saharan Africa undertake the nightmarish journey from Africa to Europe, about which I will speak later. Bouazizi did not do that for whatever reason. The choice, however, was, and still is, that between two types of nightmares: on one hand, perhaps he was destined to spark the uprising that brought down Ben Ali then Egypt's Mubarak, and others; on the other, perhaps he was destined to sacrifice himself in order to highlight (so that the whole world could see) the plight and potentiality of the Arab world from North Africa to the Middle East. Thus began a series of events that had some very positive and negative results. For the latter, Libya should suffice as an example. But there's also Egypt, where the military are back in power more brutal than ever, and Bahrain, which was defended by Saudi Arabia and the United States who were eager to crush the resistance before it became too late.

The logic of work—that is, people have to work in order to be deserving of a decent life—is used as a weapon against the class and the multitude that became known as the 99 percent during Occupy Wall Street. Of course, work also means not work, and the latter includes all life activities not acknowledged as work (e.g., housework, the work of care, art, poetry, and so on) as well as unemployment.[6] An unemployed person is a work-er (he or she who works) who does not work. It is someone who should be working but does not work. Similarly, we have the category of underemployment, which is increasingly common. It often includes people doing various and odd jobs. It is a twilight zone in which Bouazizi also found himself. It is also the border zone of migration: people forced out of their places of origin to find themselves, unemployed or underemployed, in new and usually unwelcoming countries. Together with the Arab Spring, movements in Europe such as the Indignados, and similar movements around the globe, Occupy Wall Street challenged this state of affairs and these assumptions according to which you have to work (it's an "ethical" command) whether you are employed or unemployed. In the latter case, of course, you have to try harder; constantly work in order to find work, become, as they say, your own entrepreneur; perform odd jobs here and there, and be at the mercy of the logic of debt, which can take everything from you, including your life.

As a movement against the enemy (i.e., against capital, financial capital), Occupy was or is a movement against work. Indeed, we all "aid the enemy" when we work or when we perform (formally or informally) *productive* labor that produces and increases capital. To rise against work, or to oppose it, is to liberate the creativity inherent in the ontology of labor as a neutral category, where productivity or the lack of productivity no longer counts. Labor (as productive labor) is certainly not the measure of the good life; it is rather the way by which we are compelled to give up our time, dignity, and peace of mind, as we are enslaved through debt and forced to pay for our very existence. In fact, today there is a growing awareness that existence itself should be the basis for having access to the means of subsistence, to a decent and good life, regardless of whether one works or does not work or any other determination. There has also been for some time a concrete demand for a guaranteed, or unconditional, basic income.[7] This demand is based on the notion that what used to be considered unproductive in the Fordist model of capitalist production—activities that include not only art, work, and leisure but also forms of consumption, study, and care: in one word, life itself—[8] is now productive of value. To give an example, especially in situations of illness, disability, and aging, taking care of oneself entails a lot of *work* (broadly defined) and it is productive of value. There is a specific requirement, which is made on all of us, to become entrepreneurs of the self in order to have some space and a degree of autonomy and power in what might still resemble the classic paradigm of economic life: the market and its ideal of productivity. But to narrow down and deepen our example, an aging person with various medical conditions will have to perform a lot of work on a regular basis in order to be able to take care of himself or herself. According to the logic of capitalist production, this is not productive of any value, and thus it has no value at all. In truth, this and other similar instances belong in what Carlo Vercellone calls *subterranean labor*, which is in turn part of a *compulsory nonmarket economy* (*economia non di mercato forzata;* 2006: 201). Vercellone explains, "Subterranean labor is, in the first place, non-compensated life, namely, that part of human activity that, despite fully participating in the production of wealth, is not calculated in as a value creating power" (201; my translation). This justifies the notion of an unconditional basic income both technically (i.e., from a strictly economic point of view) and ethically. Indeed, it is the awareness of the dignity of such a demand that cannot be reined in by the exploitative and oppressive system of financial capital and police terror. It is this subterranean labor that grounds the power of the 99 percent, of current movements of protest and resistance throughout the world.

Calling into question the logic of value in light of what is now known as the biopolitical model yields very interesting results. The gap between the time of work and the time of life is disappearing, and alienation is no longer perceived because it has become a constant state. Highlighting the compulsory nature of wage labor (which is formally free and voluntary but in truth *forced*), Marx says in the *Economic and Philosophical Manuscripts* that the worker "is at home when he is not working and when he is working he is not at home" (1994b: 62). Alienation, this being outside oneself and not at home, becomes permanent when work is life and life is work.

Migration is one of the most striking examples of the identity of work and life and the disappearing of the distinction between the time of life and the time of work and being at home and not being at home. Migration calls into question the existence of borders, including the border between life and work. It means alienation and homelessness. Obviously, the condition of migration can be experienced in one's own place of origin (or one's own country) either because of internal migration (actual internal displacement, as when people are forced to move away from their original areas due to war, natural disasters, and so on) or because of a type of displacement that is perhaps more subtle, less visible in its process, yet no less disruptive and destructive. The latter type is the homelessness experienced by an increasing number of people in the world's largest cities that brings about anxiety and depression, fear, and loneliness, as marginalization, unemployment, underemployment, and oppressiveness rise. The self is thus displaced. One is lost in a meaningless world with the injunction of having to go on, live and work, or try to find work and make a living in conditions that are entirely destructive of the human spirit. This was the experience of Bouazizi in Tunisia, but it is also the experience of a multitude of people throughout the world. It is a borderline experience, where extreme danger is constant.

Unlike Bouazizi, those who choose to actually migrate do not do so in ways that are less compulsory and potentially fatal. Migration, whether we think of the US-Mexico border or the crossing of the Mediterranean Sea or any other specific context, always presents the same general characteristics. It is a central moment in the friend-and-enemy logic. The migrant is the potential or actual enemy. Usually, little thought is given to the fact that forces that become irresistible and unavoidable determine migration. People lose their source of livelihood in their places of origin and their right to remain where they are. They are forced to embark on a journey whose outcome is uncertain and that all too often ends tragically. Those who make it face all kinds of violence in the new places where they try to work and build a new life. The violence goes from arrest and deportation to discrimination, exploitation, constant humiliation, and even murder. The violence is institutional as well as noninstitutional. Of course, there is a difference between legal and illegal migration, but in the context of this discussion, which does not deal with the technicalities of the law but the political and ethical issue, that difference (as well as many similar others) can be overlooked. The only thing that must be mentioned, which is a battle cry for those who defend the rights and dignity of migrants, is that the obscene, offensive notion of "illegal migrant" must be struck from thought and language. We have already seen the extent of the shortcomings of the law. Legality may coincide with morality, but all too often this is not the case. In order to have a situation in which these two spheres do coincide, the law itself must do a lot of work and try very hard. But most often the law has no interest in doing so. In fact, the interests of the law are typically already turned away from the principles of ethics and justice, as when the aim is that of protecting borders, a nation's sovereignty, and so on. The illegal immigrant is the person who has crossed the border illegally. However, this simple definition only points to a technicality of the law, which from the point of view of ethics and true justice can be either irrelevant or inaccurate. Indeed, the legitimacy of the border, any border, can always be called into question, and the very notion of border is highly problematic. Consider the US-Mexico border, in particular, the southern border of Arizona. On December 14, 2014, *Democracy Now!* ran a segment on the increasing militarization of the border there, which has adversely affected 28,000 members of the Tohono O'odham (i.e., "desert people") Nation. One of the two people interviewed by *Democracy Now!* cohost Amy Goodman was Alex Soto, a member of the Tohono O'odham Nation and a hip-hop artist. At one point during the interview, he said, "You know, growing up . . . I was always raised to know that, as O'odham, . . . the land on both sides of the so-called U.S.-Mexico border is our land. And so, when I was young, there was no border there, other than chicken-wire fence for ranching or, you know, practices within the community."[9] What is true of the border is also true of the state, the nation, in general. Soto also points out the changes in immigration policy that happened in the 1980s and 1990s, especially with the passage of the North American Free Trade Agreement (NAFTA) on January 1, 1994, and how those changes affected the movement of migration and his community. He stresses the importance of the role of the global economic and political forces in shaping and determining migration.

When there are no borders and no states (a "when" that obviously points to a utopia—that is, a "not yet" but a concrete utopia), people would not only be free to move from place to place, but more important, they would be able to stay in the place of their choice (most likely their place of origin) without being chased away, having their land invaded and occupied, and having their community plagued by a culture of fear and violence. The institutional kind of violence that sets in is analogous to the violence of gangs and organized crime to the point that it is difficult to say which is more original, which mimics and reproduces the other. Those who undertake the journey of migration under forced conditions are the ones particularly threatened by both types of violence. This situation is excellently portrayed in the movie *Sin Nombre* (2009) written and directed by Cary Joji Fukunaga. The movie describes the journey of Central American migrants through Mexico to the United States. It also describes the everyday life activities of a clique (stationed in Chiapas, Mexico) of the Mara Salvatrucha (or MS-13), one of the world's most notorious gangs. In addition to the many difficulties and dangers of the journey, the migrants also face the gang's violence. Among the many interesting aspects of this great movie, there is one I want to highlight: the question of territory and border according to the gang's logic—or the logic of all gangs for that matter. A few MS-13 members are chasing El Casper (or Willy), the main character in the movie, because he has killed the gang leader, Lil Mago, trying to protect a young migrant woman from him. During the chase, they find themselves in a rival gang's territory. They in turn are chased and shot at until they cross the border and leave their rivals' territory. Perhaps we can detect the friend-and-enemy logic at its best. In a sense, there is more coherence and authenticity in the conduct of gangs than that of political entities such as the nation. Honor is certainly an essential value in both, and treason is the worst thing a member could do. The gang, however, is more forthcoming and transparent about its way of thinking and the violence that supports it. There is no doubt that violence is the way to deal with virtually every situation in life, including the rite of initiation. On the contrary, the law of the state hides its violent roots; the nation conceals its bloody origins. Reducing the question to the distinction between legality and illegality does not help, for the distinction itself is a product anticipated in the intentions and interests of the law that are always particularistic in character—unless of course one thinks of international law, whose aspiration is universal and thus in principle approximates ethics. The question is rather one of humanity—for instance, the humanity of migrants or, to stay with the illustration in *Sin Nombre*, of Willy who demonstrates the power of ethical thinking when he breaks off the gang's mentality, moral code, and so on. It is a peculiar demonstration, for in order to be ethical, he has to kill Lil Mago. The latter had killed Willy's girlfriend, so at first sight, this might appear as an act of revenge. However, despite his obvious hate and resentment for Lil Mago at that point, Willy kills him in order to defend another potential victim of his violence, Sayra, a Honduran woman who is traveling north with her father and uncle. Here, humanity is, as everywhere, not an abstract and empty concept, but a singular contraction. It becomes visible, tangible, and concrete in the situation at hand, not as an essence in political (humanitarian) discourse or a rhetorical figure but as an actual existent.

On May 15, 2014, the fast-food industry workers conducted strikes in New York City, other cities in the United States, and worldwide. The strike is for a living wage and a union. The income disparity between fast-food workers and CEOs is, as one would have expected, offensive. It has been revealed that a CEO makes around 1,200 times as much as a worker does. Where fast-food workers often work for the minimum wage of $7.25 an hour, the CEO of McDonald's makes $9,200 an hour.[10] It is in this disparity that we find the meaning and measure of the relationship between humanity and its enemy. This is indeed the meaning of class antagonism, "in a word, the oppressor and the oppressed," say Marx and Engels in *The Communist Manifesto* (1994: 15). Although the issue of wages is not the most radical—for "wages are only a necessary consequence of the alienation of labor" and they are determined by private property with which they are in a relationship of identity or symmetry—it still represents the inequality that is not only economic in a narrow sense but also political and ontological. Indeed, wages represent the way in which workers are at one and the same time included in and excluded from production under the capitalist regime. They produce yet they are excluded from

LABOR, POVERTY, AND MIGRATION

the control of the productive activity and the result of production—that is, social wealth, which is appropriated by the oppressive class of CEOs and the like. As Marx says in a colorful passage from the *Economic and Philosophic Manuscripts*, "Labor produces marvels for the wealthy but it produces deprivation for the worker. It produces palaces, but hovels for the worker. It produces beauty, but mutilation for the worker. It displaces labor through machines, but it throws some workers back into barbarous labor and turns others into machines. It produces intelligence, but for the worker it produces imbecility and cretinism" (1994b: 61).

This is the problem of alienation, described by Marx in the section on alienated labor of the *Economic and Philosophic Manuscripts*. Today, when work has virtually become identical with life, the phenomenon of alienation is ever more present, and the feeling of being at home is becoming more difficult and rare even when one is physically at home, in one's own dwelling, and in one's space, for the occupation and subsumption of all time and space under the regime of obsessive productivity and growth have become total. This is of course true of the digital economy, which includes not only those actually working in information technology and actually sitting in front of a computer screen but also virtually everybody, for everybody is directly or indirectly impacted by it. Thus a new form of alienation presents itself, whereby the worker is not at home even when he or she is at home. However, this is not a situation from which there is no exit.

In a recent, interesting reformulation of the problem of alienation, Franco Berardi (2009) distinguishes between the type of alienation I have been describing earlier and the active, creative estrangement that breaks free of it and thus posits a new ontology, new future possibilities. Berardi goes back to Italian "workerism" (which he renames "compositionism"), which he says, "[P]resents the issue of alienation in radically different terms than those of humanism" (44). He makes clear that there is here no "restoration of humanity" and no "human universality," for humanity is understood in terms of "class conflict" (ibid.). I agree. However, the humanity that emerges from class conflict is the only humanity, and thus it retains a claim to universality. When I say this, I am not advancing the notion of the restoration of a human essence, which I grant does not exist, but rather the idea of the human condition. This is a condition in which potentialities can be fully developed and starting from which the good life could be attainable. But the truth is that for a growing number of people, this has become impossible. They are driven back into conditions that are less than human or completely inhuman. A "restoration" (I prefer a "return") that is universal in character is thus in order. It is not the war of humanity against the inhuman but rather the revolutionary, class-based destruction of the preconditions of war. Those who like to oppress, exploit, and wage war against others must be diminished and isolated, and their power must be deactivated. This is the only cultural, counterhegemonic force that can drive them back into the nothingness from which they have risen. That the present system of oppression and violence must be destroyed is beyond doubt. The question is how to do so.

Berardi says, and I quote him approvingly, "It is precisely thanks to the radical inhumanity of the workers' existence that a human collectivity can be founded, a community no longer dependent on capital" (ibid.). This radical inhumanity is indeed the only human community, the only humanity. There is no other. Those who like to preach in the name of humanity, humanism, human rights, humanitarianism, and so on simply do that: preach—in ways that are most hypocritical and insulting. This is what the United States, the imperial power, and more generally, the West have been doing with particular zeal in the last decades to say the least. However, this is no reason to forsake the name of humanity, which precisely names the *radical inhumanity* of the oppressed. It is instead a name that must be reappropriated and used as a powerful weapon against the oppressor, the enemy of humanity. The logic of capital alienates humanity (the workers), and humanity becomes inhuman. This is clear from Marx's pages on alienated labor, where "*a man other than the worker*" (1994b: 65; emphasis in the original) appears as the owner of both labor and the product of labor. The worker is othered by this other who has the legal and political power to appropriate all humanness, all humanity. He or she is confined to the inhuman condition, where no flourishing and no good or decent life are possible—perhaps no life at all other than biological passivity. However, this radical inhumanity is also a reversal and a return—a refusal and thus the spring of the revolution. Berardi says, "It is indeed the estrangement of the workers from their labor, the feeling of alienation and its refusal, that are the bases for a human collectivity autonomous from capital" (2009: 44–45). This is the positive dimension of the whole situation: "Workers do not suffer from their alienation when they can transform it into active estrangement, that is to say, into refusal" (46). The refusal to submit to wage labor lays the foundation for "a community that is aware and free, cohesive and erotic" (115). Wage labor is the enemy: the system of capital, war, and global dominance. Humanity is the coming community: the family, friendship, and love.

This refusal is not a right inscribed in the double (thus formal and empty) freedom of the worker. Rather, it is a moral duty in the sense in which disobedience and resistance always are, for working under the oppressive regime of capital has the meaning of not only "aiding the enemy" but participating in one's own dehumanization. To become a commodity, a thing, and "an appendage of the machine" (Marx and Engels 1994: 164) means to no longer be human. The loss of humanity is individual and collective, particular and universal. However, it is the notion of universality that in particular interests us here, for it is one too often attacked or simply dismissed according to an antihumanist posture, which is in itself rather problematic. So I want to point out that Marx's description of the proletariat is precisely one of a universal class, whose universality lies in the dissolution of all classes, including of itself as a class. It is not because of any sense of loyalty toward Marx that this should be kept in mind, but rather because it seems to still be a very important and timely thought. Thus for Marx the proletariat is "a class that is the dissolution of all classes, a sphere of society having a universal character because of its universal suffering and claiming no *particular* right because no *particular wrong* but *unqualified wrong* is perpetrated on it" (1994a: 38). Earlier, when I say that the loss of humanity is individual and collective, particular and universal, I am not contradicting what Marx says; obviously, the proletariat remains a particular class, as Marx also says at the end of the paragraph from which I am quoting, and it is made of individual human beings. What is important, and must be stressed, is the fact that *universal suffering* characterizes it. Marx continues his description of the proletariat saying that it is "a sphere that can invoke no *traditional* title but only a *human* title . . . ; finally, that cannot emancipate itself without emancipating itself from all other spheres of society, thereby emancipating them; a sphere, in short, that is the *complete loss* of humanity and can only redeem itself through the *total redemption of humanity*" (ibid.). One can complain about the *essentialism* in Marx here; obviously, for him there is a restoration of humanity. However, I do not see that as a problem, for what must be restored starting from this *radical inhumanity* is the condition of its flourishing. In other words, the issue is not the restoration of a preestablished and fixed nature, which for Marx does not exist, but the radical transformation of *relations* capable of producing total human emancipation and the conditions for universal happiness. The issue is that of an alternative and radical ontology of the human, and also the nonhuman. Today, we can understand the proletariat described by Marx as the 99 percent, to use the language of Occupy Wall Street, or as the precariat, the new and growing sphere of society, which is and is not of society, included in and excluded from the contemporary mode of production, sustained by nothing but its capacity to constantly reproduce and reinvent itself, create itself in a constantly alienating and alienated mode, through a constant and exhausting effort, under the obligation to see life as work, or life as debt—and death.[11] Indeed, as we quickly move toward a *jobless future*,[12] precarity becomes the dominant and universal condition in which the radical inhumanity inscribed in the material and moral obligation to work, to see life as work, and to constantly have to look for new ways of surviving becomes absolutely evident. The proletariat, 99 percent, or precariat, becomes the only possible configuration of humanity; it becomes identical with humanity. It is in this sense that humanity itself becomes a political subject, the revolutionary subject, against the radical inhumanity in which it is forced. The system is its enemy—the system of capital and its global character, of the state and its ideological and repressive apparatuses. And this system must be dismantled and demolished.

In *The Communist Manifesto*, Marx and Engels wrote, "The proletarian movement is the self-conscious, independent movement of the immense majority, in the interest of the immense majority" (1994: 168). This is even truer today, with the understanding that this *immense majority* is humanity itself. Whatever the tiny minority might be, the 1 percent and their guards, they do not partake in the *interest* (understood as being-between) of humanity in a proper sense because they have set themselves apart from it. For them, interest is only a matter of finance, just like freedom is only a matter of free trade—that is, the freedom to exploit and oppress, dominate and plunder. With them, all violence resides. The "self-conscious, independent movement" of resistance, which is the same as the subjective, autonomous constitution of humanity as a political subject (the subject of a new politics, inextricably linked to ethics), is not the violence that ends all violence, the war that ends all wars, but it is rather the end of violence and war and the beginning of more enlightened and sophisticated ways to look at reality, live life, and understand the world. Many have complained that the Arab Spring was not organized and Occupy Wall Street (and the Occupy movement in general) had no program. However, what both movements highlighted is the need and desire for something new, an alternative to the thoughtless and stubborn logic of the enemy. Their insight, despite the brutal repression of the powers that be, remains alive, perhaps at a subterranean level, and it will surface once again. Indeed, there is no reason to believe that humanity, "the immense majority," has been defeated once and for all. On the contrary, the system will soon have to sustain a counterattack from which it will not be able to recover because it will proceed from the ontological plane of its formation, showing its failure as well as the ethical foundation of the world to come. This is the meaning of class conflict today: the difference between two ways of thinking, modes of desire and subjectification.

Let me give two examples, which come from personal observation. One has to do with the changes taking place in some areas of Calabria, in southern Italy, and the other with the situation in Lampedusa. They both have to do with the issues of labor, poverty, migration, and the making of an alternative—and a powerful one. In January 2010, a migrant revolt broke out in and around Rosarno, Calabria. Fed up with the systemic exploitation to which they were constantly exposed, African migrants from North Africa and especially sub-Saharan Africa took to the streets and rebelled against the racist and oppressive work and life conditions they had to endure.[13] They are seasonal workers who live and work in the Rosarno area during the orange-picking season and then move to other areas throughout Italy in search of new opportunities to sustain themselves. They live in abandoned, run-down rural houses or in tent cities that are regularly destroyed by the state at the end of the working season.[14] Since 2010, their conditions are miserable and appalling and they are very poor. However, the 2010 revolt opened up a space for the constitution of an ethical and political community that unites the migrants and the noncompliant, radical, and revolutionary, locals. SOS Rosarno was born, an organization that since then has done a lot to try to redress the injustice at both an ideological and material level.[15] Although the situation is beyond what even an organization like SOS Rosarno can solve, the positing of a potential alternative remains very strong. Even as of January 2014, when I visited the area, the majority of migrants remained in a state that was absolutely inhuman. The tent city near Rosarno hosted thousands of people when it could only host a few hundreds. They lived in extreme poverty and unsanitary conditions with no running water or electricity and with garbage and waste scattered throughout the camp. Yet at the same time, a network was built that has had an impact on both the material and cultural levels of everyday life. Through a joint effort with cooperatives like I Frutti del Sole (fruits of the sun) and other realities on the ground, SOS Rosarno has been able to challenge the apathy of the Rosarno area marred by a longtime 'Ndrangheta-dominated subculture.[16] Although the situation remains dire for most, some migrants are now hired at union wages, and this seems to be a growing tendency. SOS Rosarno and I Frutti del Sole have embraced a strict fair-trade policy and a type of organic agricultural production. They operate outside the logic of large-scale distribution in collaboration with a network of Solidarity Purchase Groups (Gruppi di Acquisto Solidale, or GAS).[17] In a recent fight with COOP, a large and well-established distribution network of consumers' cooperatives in Italy, SOS Rosarno and I Frutti del Sole have argued that what is essential is not only that the product be organic but also that its value (and thus its price) take into account the labor that goes into it, and thus the humanity of workers. This means that a fair share of the price must go to the worker—that is, the migrant worker. The challenge here is not only economic but also political and cultural (indeed, ethical and human) in character. As long as money remains the means of subsistence, it must be made available to everyone—though of course money remains a peculiar expression and a reflection of something that reaches into the ontology of social being: existence, labor, and time. The point I am making here is that even in a relatively backward area like Calabria, afflicted by centuries of abandonment and deprivation, something new is emerging—a new self-consciousness and new objective potentialities—due to the global changes that bring about disruption of old modes of life as well as conditions for a future world of cooperation, solidarity, and peace.

The second example is about Lampedusa, a tiny and beautiful island in the Mediterranean Sea, off the coast of Tunisia. Belonging geographically to Africa but politically to Italy, Lampedusa has become one of the main ports of entry to Europe for many African migrants. They undertake the perilous journey across the Mediterranean leaving from Libya, where they often arrive after a similarly dangerous journey across the Sahara and where they are often abused, imprisoned, and tortured. Finally, they find themselves in the hands of cynical human smugglers, who very often leave them to their own fate in the open sea. Hans

Lucht notes, "How many people have died trying to cross the Mediterranean is unclear" (2012: 120).[18] In one of the worst tragedies, on October 3, 2013, close to four hundred people died when a fishing boat carrying over five hundred people caught on fire and then capsized in the waters near Lampedusa. They were people from Eritrea, Ethiopia, Somalia, Ghana, and Tunisia. On October 11, 2013, another shipwreck in the waters between Malta and Lampedusa resulted in 268 deaths. This time it was people from Syria escaping the violence that is destroying their country. Subsequently, the Mediterranean became increasingly militarized. The Italian navy will now intercept fishing boats arriving from Libya on the high sea before they get to Lampedusa, identify the migrants, and send them to detention centers throughout Italy or back to Libya and other countries. Even those who are not sent back become the victims of a vicious policy, for, having been fingerprinted and identified in Italian territory, they will in the future not be able to move to other European countries,[19] which is what most migrants who arrive in Lampedusa and Italy desire.

A blog entry by the Askavusa Collective (which I will discuss more next) says, "After the shipwrecks of October 3 and October 11, Europe has militarized the Mediterranean and the island of Lampedusa in a massive way" (my translation).[20] Then the blog article gives the history of the series of states of emergency and the steady tendency toward total militarization starting from the Council of the European Union's creation of Frontex in 2004. Frontex stands for European Agency for the Management of Operational Cooperation at the External Borders of the Member States of the European Union. As many now recognize, the real aim of Frontex is the creation of "Fortress Europe," inaccessible to what is deemed to be "irregular" migration.

The cost of all this is not only on the migrants who are detained, imprisoned, sent back to Libya or their country of origin, or in any case, exploited and oppressed in Europe but also on those—like the people of Lampedusa—who find themselves caught in an unbearable situation. Having become a global metaphor, Lampedusa is now completely under the control of the most sophisticated and cynical military power. The island is used and abused for the sake of political interests that have nothing to do with its rhythm, its sense of everyday life, and its construction of happiness. At the end of January 2014, more than fifty organizations from all over Europe (social movements, activists, and nongovernmental organizations, among others) met on the island for the drafting of the Lampedusa Charter. However, despite the excellent points made by the charter (which for a question of space I cannot discuss here),[21] the point remains that Lampedusa and its people were used for aims that are not necessarily transparent and are certainly not breaking with the usual logic of institutional politics—ultimately, the friend-and-enemy logic. It is for this reason that the Askavusa Collective chose not to participate in the drafting of the charter.

Askavusa ("barefoot") is a collective in Lampedusa. They do political, social, and cultural work. When I visited Lampedusa toward the end of January 2014, they were in the process of opening their new location, Porto M, which is also a place where the memory of the migrants who died and those who made it to the shore and moved forward in their journey toward Europe is kept alive. The front of Porto M is covered with pieces from the boats recovered from the boat cemetery in the new port of Lampedusa. Inside Porto M, there are all kinds of objects belonging to the migrants: clothes, marine equipment such as life vests and rope, notebooks used as travelogues, and so on. This is indeed an invaluable historical and artistic work—a process that looks at the history of the present and the

kind of art that is not separate from everyday life. Just like
with SOS Rosarno in Calabria, there is a full recuperation
of the notion and reality of the human condition here.
There is also a reiteration of Hölderlin's famous lines from
"Patmos": "Yet where the danger lies, / Grows that which
saves" (1984: 89). There is a clear vision enhanced by
the North African colors bathing the island: that another
world is possible, a world of justice, happiness, and peace.
When I said to Giacomo Sferlazzo of the Askavusa Collective that what they envision and do sounds like a utopia,
he replied, "It is a utopia."

CHAPTER 5

DEACTIVATING TERROR
AND THE ENEMY LOGIC

In a short essay called "Sovereign Police," Giorgio Agamben writes, "The sovereigns who willingly agreed to present themselves as cops or executioners, in fact, now show in the end their original proximity to the criminal" (2000: 107). This citation by Agamben can be used to address the question of the "apparatus" (*dispositif*)[1] within which a double imaginary plays a pivotal role. Thus we have two types of imaginary. One is the imaginary tending to the defense of the status quo; it is, in fact, the sovereign imaginary, the imaginary of the police and the sovereign police, of debt and death, of exchange value, and of the total privatization and financialization of life. This is the imaginary for which the apparatus of repression and of production of new and better forms of subjection must be perfected and refined: new forms of discipline, punishment, and prepunishment. The other is the imaginary of liberation exemplified by, among other recent situations, the Occupy movement, which has sought the dismantling and destruction of the repressive and coercive dominant apparatus (or system).

Following Michel Foucault, I will try to describe a strategic rather than dialectical logic, and I will try to show that ultimately it is the autonomy of the imagination and will to liberation, rather than their dialogical and dialectical encounter with a rotten system of domination, that may turn into an actual reality what has for so long been the cry and program of progressive thinking and practice under the slogan "Another world is possible."

In the second lecture of *The Birth of Biopolitics*, Foucault distinguishes between dialectical and strategic logic. He says, "Dialectical logic puts to work contradictory terms within the homogeneous. I suggest replacing this dialectical logic with what I would call a strategic logic. A logic of strategy does not stress contradictory terms within a homogeneity that promises their resolution in a unity. The function of strategic logic is to establish the possible connections between disparate terms which remain disparate. The logic of strategy is the logic of connections between the heterogeneous and not the logic of the homogenization of the contradictory" (2004: 42).

From the point of view of dialectical logic, of the homogeneous and its potential unity, a social and political struggle will hardly lead to liberation, but it will rather lead to a return of sort to what now appears to be a new condition, where the sublated terms are still present in their apparent absence, but essentially present; neither has gone over into the other, neither has been eliminated. On the contrary, the heterogeneity of strategic logic allows for spaces of alterity. What is named here is not *another* whose destiny is assimilation into a (new) one but a simple other, *one-other-than*, that has no destiny (or necessity) but is pure contingency. This is also what the notion of dignity of individuation I formulated in *Earthly Plenitudes* (Gullì 2010) names: a singularity.

To be sure, in the passage I cited earlier, Foucault is not saying that strategic logic is necessarily, or primarily, a logic of liberation. In fact, he is saying that it is the logic of liberalism, whereby various apparatuses or *dispositifs* are found in a situation of tension and friction with one another.[2] However, precisely because of the heterogeneous character of the relation, the multiplicity involved therein, there remains the possibility that struggle and war may create spaces of irreducible alterity. As Maurizio Lazzarato explains, sometimes "the government plays one dispositif against the other; sometimes it relies on one, sometimes on the other." And that is, for instance, the juridical, economic, or social dispositif.[3] However, precisely because *the governed* are not involved in a dialectical (or dialogical) relation tending to a unity, but are rather left, subjected, in the facticity of being "object[s] of information, never . . . subject[s] in communication" (Foucault 1977: 200), they can, precisely on that account, start and implement strategies other than those of the established apparatuses, whereby the latter ruin and collapse. This is precisely what has been happening with the Occupy movement, where clashing with the police, for instance, is of course not the aim. The clashes are, as we have seen in the previous chapter, the result of a unilateral type of violence, unleashed by the government itself, exercised by ill-advised and thoughtless (and often extremely vicious) police officers.

This violence is of course not the result of a secret maneuver of a few people in high governmental positions but rather the expression of a network of apparatuses (including the police in the narrow sense), which tries to create and maximize a degree of consensus among the subjected population in addition to legitimizing the dirty work of control and surveillance, intimidation, and repression. To this purpose, nothing works better than the rhetoric of the need for security from the threat of terror—a rhetoric totally supported and duly disseminated by mainstream media. This is not to say that those who manage to get to high positions of power (from the president or prime minister of a nation to its attorney general to the mayors of cities large and small, etc.) have nothing to do with this. As I have noted, the violence we are experiencing is unleashed by the leading governments themselves. However, these "leaders" are only willful (and superficial) agents of forms of coercion and repression, whose origin is more systemic and structural. These original forms are themselves nothing but a usurpation of a totally different power, usually referred to as the power of the people. Many people would not agree with this description, but I think that a strong argument can be made to show that we are dealing with forms of usurpation of a more fundamental, and essentially different, power. Those who would disagree would probably say that institutional positions of power are, at least in our "democratic" society, occupied by elected officials or other people appointed by the elected officials. These positions of power ultimately rest on that celebrated principle of the power of the people. But everybody knows that this is utterly false, because the separation between the government and the governed, which is a mark of sovereignty, is such that what should be power *of* the people turns into powerlessness, subjectivity turns to subjection, freedom to unfreedom, and communication to the facticity of surveillance and control. Moreover, the very concept of the people today is called into question and rightly so by the theorists of the multitude,[4] for the people is *one* only in relation to the sovereign sign, and thus as soon as its power is falsely posited in the phrase "the power of the people," it is also taken away by the assimilation of the many (concrete people) into the unity of a totally imaginary one, which is the one crushed under the sovereign sign: "one nation under God," the highest and most accomplished sovereign.

Speaking of sovereignty may be a bit problematic here because I am making use of some categories from Foucault. In fact, Foucault distinguishes between the modality of sovereignty and more general forms of domination, which take the place of sovereignty or coexist with it (Foucault 1997). However, I think that all forms of domination have a regard for the logic of sovereignty, an anticipation or residue of it. Moreover, I think that lately, despite the crisis of sovereignty at the level of the politics of states and international relations (i.e., the Westphalian model of sovereignty), we are witnessing a newly arising form of it, precisely in the sense of Agamben's notion of the sovereign police. But sovereign police means not only that policing now happens on a global scale (i.e., that heads of state can be arrested, removed, and executed, as highlighted by Agamben) but—as I hope I have shown in Chapter 3—that the police everywhere retain the trait of the sovereign and use and abuse it along with their batons, guns, pepper spray, and water cannons. The two aspects of the sovereign police come together in a very interesting and clear way in the assassination program launched by George W. Bush and escalated and enhanced by the Obama administration. We now know that Barack Obama, today's most powerful sovereign on earth, is "personally involved" in the assassination program and picks and chooses from a kill list.[5]

Before addressing the assassination program more closely, I would like to remark on something that Foucault says in *The Birth of Biopolitics*, while he is himself remarking on aspects of his own book *Discipline and Punish*. In discussing the new governmental reason, "interested in interests," a thing that follows from the logic of strategy I discussed previously, Foucault gives a brief synopsis of what is one of the main theses in *Discipline and Punish*: the change in the penal system in the eighteenth and nineteenth centuries from punishment as the direct intervention of the sovereign (hence torture and execution) to the "principle of mildness in punishment . . . which, once again, was not the expression of something like a change in people's sensibility" (2004: 46–47). In *Discipline and Punish*, in a chapter called "Generalized Punishment,"

Foucault says, "The reform of criminal law must be read as a *strategy* for the rearrangement of the power to punish, according to modalities that render it more regular, more effective, more constant and more detailed in its effects; in short, which increase its effects while diminishing its economic cost . . . and its political cost" (1977: 80–81; emphasis added).

The point was "not to punish less, but to punish better" (82). Foucault had already previously noted in the text, and he will again later in the same chapter, that the idea was that punishment should replace revenge (74, 90), which was the modality typical of the direct and personal intervention of the sovereign being now superseded by a new strategy in criminal justice for the sake of the defense of society: "It became necessary to define a *strategy* and techniques of punishment in which an economy of continuity and permanence would replace that of expenditure and excess" (87; emphasis added).

The last two words in the previous passage obviously bring to mind Georges Bataille for whom sovereignty was precisely "expenditure" and "excess"—namely, that which does not serve. Bataille has a curious way of ultimately assigning sovereignty a potentially revolutionary character.[6] Perhaps even more important is to note that the new economy of continuity and permanence—that is, the new strategy of normalization replacing the sovereign modality of vengeance—also implies the end of the *exception*, which is the sovereign's most characteristic trait, as Carl Schmitt (2005) famously stressed. This is why Foucault speaks of *generalized* punishment, which of course includes all possible forms of prepunishment and collective punishment.

Going back to the present role and practice of the sovereign police in our societies at the global and local levels, there seem to be some interesting questions arising. First, is there a regression today to previous and obsolete forms

of power, punishment, and control? Have these forms perhaps never been superseded? Or is there (and has there
been all along) a combination of the old and the new (i.e.,
new and more efficient strategies and techniques) but
coupled with the old sovereign right to punish and take
revenge? I have a sense that the last question can give us
an insight into what the situation truly is today. First of all,
it supports the idea that there is anticipation, or a residue,
of sovereignty in domination as such; in other words, the
sign of sovereignty is still impressed and visible everywhere.
But it also says that, if Foucault's analysis has any value—
and I think it does indeed have great value—old forms
of power that seemed to be fading (and Foucault never
says they had completely disappeared) are perhaps today
gaining new strength for reasons that must be explained.
One reason might be that a gasping power, one that has
dominance without hegemony (Arrighi 2010 and 2007),[7]
needs to revert to forms that had at one point in time
perhaps become unnecessary and even useless while at the
same time devise new forms to make sure it is still in charge
and in control. Thus the sovereign intervention may take
on the form of a drone (a remotely piloted aircraft) today
while it refines the machinery of control and surveillance
with more sophisticated and refined techniques by opaque
agencies, such as the National Security Agency (NSA), or
even the New York Police Department (NYPD; e.g., one
may think of the recent news about the NYPD surveillance of Muslim people and businesses miles away from its
jurisdiction [in New Jersey and Connecticut]). Moreover,
the police intervene in a sovereign manner. This means
that they do not simply intervene in the typical role and
function of the police, but they intervene from the site
of absolute and supreme power typical of the sovereign
and according to the sovereign's modalities of intimidation and vengeance. We see this every time people take to
the streets to protest all over the world: the Arab Spring,

the Indignados in Europe, the fast-food industry workers, and many other situations of opposition to regimes of
violence everywhere. In the United States, this has regularly been the case since the Occupy movement started
in September 2011—though it might be interesting to
note that some eight months before that, during the Wis-
consin Uprising, the police had joined the protest. Again,
the action of the police is sovereign in all cases of police
brutality, which are increasing exponentially and becoming more and more vicious and appalling. It is also worth
noting that police abuse of power does not start with
episodes of brutality, but with the very intimidating and
aggressive presence of the police, whether it be at political
demonstrations and rallies or in the city's everyday life,
especially of course in some areas of the city (e.g., inner
cities, ghettos, or the favelas) chosen for special measures
of surveillance, repression, and control according to a racist logic of violence. What becomes apparent is that it is
not the case that a regime of the norm has replaced the
sovereign regime of the exception but rather the exception has become the norm, and consequently, the sign of
sovereignty is now everywhere.

The ubiquity of sovereignty, of the sovereign police, (and
here police should be understood in its broadest sense) is
easily seen in the culture of impunity and unaccountability
that certainly after 9/11 engulfed the world. There are clear
signs of this at the global level (drone strikes) as well as at
the local level (police arrogance and brutality).[8] That there
is sovereignty, rather than simply unsovereign domination,
should be clear from the very meaning of "impunity" and
"unaccountability," as well as from their place in theology,
where the doctrine of sovereignty originates. Typically, God
is not accountable to anyone.

The institutional attempts at justifying and legitimizing the usurpation and abuse of power inscribed in the
formula of sovereignty and domination do not convince

anyone. We hear about these attempts every time the spokesperson for a city's police department or for the State Department, after an episode of police brutality, a massacre, or other atrocities in a war zone, says that "[t]his is not who we are or what we stand for." In other words, the brutal episode in question is brushed away as an isolated case, a mistake, and so on. Other times, without blushing at the blatant contradiction, we hear *in full transparency* that this is indeed who we are and what we stand for. In other words, the use of excessive force is justified by the situation on the ground. Think for instance of when John Brennan, then-chief counterterrorism advisor to President Obama, informed the American people that it is true that "the United States Government conducts targeted strikes against specific al-Qaeda terrorists, sometimes using remotely piloted aircrafts, often referred to publicly as drones."[9]

Of course, he does not say that these "terrorists" are very often regular and innocent people (at times children) or insurgents and rebels. He insists that all is lawful, and he stresses that it is in accordance with international law. Before saying that "[t]argeted strikes are wise," he lays out the four principles to which said strikes conform: the principles of necessity, distinction, and proportionality are the first three principles. The principle of necessity requires "that the targets have definite military value," but of course the determination of value is always a very tricky matter. The principle of distinction is very reasonable, for it simply says that "only military objectives may be intentionally targeted and that civilians are protected from being intentionally targeted." I think that anyone would agree that the distinction between military objectives and civilians is an important one, and it should be a clear-cut distinction, although this goes back to the question of the definition of value, as per the first principle. In fact, it is difficult to understand why it was even made into a principle if it were not for the telling repetition of the word *intentionally*. Obviously, "protected from being intentionally targeted" does not entail protected from being targeted. The principle of proportionality is very interesting. It says that "the anticipated collateral damage of an action cannot be excessive in relation to the anticipated military advantage." Strictly understood, this principle would disqualify many military actions as legitimate actions. For instance, on the basis of such a principle, one would not have dropped the atomic bombs on Hiroshima and Nagasaki, or perhaps one would have, for proportionality is a very relative concept, since it always depends on how many American lives are involved. So the first three principles all have nice names, especially the first two—necessity and distinction—with their obvious philosophical connotation. But even proportionality has its merit, especially due to the reflexive manner of its formulation. Yet the best principle is the fourth one: the principle of humanity, "which requires us to use weapons that will not inflict unnecessary suffering."[10] Here, Foucault's account of the change in punishment comes back in full force. The public and spectacular execution with whose account *Discipline and Punish* begins—the torture, dismemberment and quartering of Robert-François Damiens, the regicide (who in any case had not succeeded in killing the king)—would certainly be a poor model for our principle of humanity. A drone fits the principle much better, because it is faster, somewhat cleaner, more efficient, and certainly removed from direct view and experience. It may be captured on a camera and reproduced on the screen, especially the destruction and ruin after the strike. "The spectators," we ourselves, can still be "edified" (I am repeating some words from the account of the Damiens execution given by a publication of the time, 1757, and cited by Foucault at the outset of *Discipline and Punish*). What is important is that there is no *unnecessary suffering*, as that would be a savagery and a bestiality that we leave to the terrorists. After all, this is not who we are or what we stand for. The paragraph containing the principle of humanity, no doubt the highest of the four principles, ends as follows: "For these reasons, I suggest to you that these targeted strikes against al-Qaeda terrorists are indeed *ethical and just*"[11] (emphasis added). They are just because these people are terrorists, so we are justified in killing them; they are also ethical because, even in terrorists, we respect the principle of humanity. In other words, as usual, we are good and they are evil. And we are exceptionally good, perhaps infinitely good, for we are capable of great acts of kindness even to the ones who are exceptionally or infinitely evil. What the self-legitimizing sovereign discourse omits to say is that the drone strikes are terrorist acts in their own right. Brennan's speech is not different from the speeches we often hear from Prime Minister Benjamin Netanyahu and other Israeli officials in defense of their ongoing murderous attacks on the Palestinian people or from the speeches of any other regime that looks at its population as raw material to be controlled and disciplined or as bare life to be regulated by increasingly sophisticated techniques of biopower.

We can then go back to the Agamben quotation I used at the outset of this chapter: "The sovereigns who willingly agreed to present themselves as cops or executioners, in fact, now show in the end their original proximity to the criminal" (2000: 107). The statement is not saying that the sovereign (e.g., the corrupt sovereign) is capable of criminal acts. Instead, the idea is that the sovereign is an *outlaw* according to its "original" meaning. The sovereign is an outlaw because he is above the law. He is above the law insofar as he is the lawmaker. Being himself the law, the sovereign seems to coincide with the limit, touching on the inside, *deciding* about the inside, and yet having absolute access to the outside—that is, an access denied to those who remain (trapped) within the sovereign web. But truly, the sovereign is not the limit; he is this open and absolute access to what lies beyond the limit, which he establishes at will and on the basis of mere violence or the threat of violence.

It is this situation that all revolutionary movements challenge. The limit must go and the separation must be exploded. The sovereign is useless and harmful (a useless burden, a harmful parasite). The radical imagination shatters the logic of inside and outside. Its strategy exposes sovereign violence. More than simply nonviolent in a generic sense (i.e., where nonviolence seems to imply a notion of passive submission, if not an act of compliance), the strategy seems to be close to what Antonio Gramsci described as a *war of position*. Gramsci famously distinguished between a war of position and a war of maneuver. The latter happens when the revolutionary movement has the capacity to overpower the dominant (though perhaps no longer hegemonic) system: the state, its police, and so on. The former has the (perhaps hidden and surprising) capacity to let the system fall of its own accord. This means that the system *does and does not* fall of its own accord. It does fall of its own accord insofar as no direct and physical blow is exerted on it; yet it does not insofar as without the war of position it would endure and linger in its fetid putrescence. It is in this sense that one speaks of nonviolence, though it is really what Walter Benjamin paradoxically (and problematically) calls *sovereign violence* (1978: 300). This unviolent violence, which is "sovereign" because it deactivates the mechanism (or apparatus) of the limit, is nothing but the individuation of dignity, which is in turn the condition for the possibility of a prosperous, peaceful, and common humanity. Another way of addressing this would be to call it counterviolence, following Frantz Fanon (2004). Deactivating the mechanism of violence—that is, sovereign (or divine) violence, which is "lethal without spilling blood" (Benjamin 1978: 297)—clears the ground for a new ontology and a new history of humankind. It *counters* violence in the most essential way, for it destroys it. It is then *counter*violence in the strictest, most literal sense: a standing against whereby that against which it stands falls of its own accord and is thus deactivated and neutralized.

Indeed, the violence that characterized the twentieth century, and virtually all known human history before that, seems to have entered the twenty-first century with exceptional force and singularity. It is true that this century opened with the terrible events of September 11. However, September 11 is not the beginning of history. Nor are the histories of more forgotten places and people and the events that shape those histories less terrible and violent, though they may often be less spectacular. Of course, many have noted the tragic coincidence between September 11, 2001, and the first (i.e., "the other") September 11: Chile, 1973. On that day, the democratically elected government of socialist Salvador Allende was violently overthrown by a military coup backed by the CIA.[12] The singularity of this violence, this paradigm of terror, does not even simply lie in its globality, for that is something that our century shares with the whole history of capitalism and empire of which it is a part. Rather, it must be seen in the fact that terror as a global phenomenon has now become self-conscious. However, this self-consciousness—of a divided self, to be sure—is grounded in despair.

At the outset of *Hopes and Prospects*, one of his latest books, Noam Chomsky says that "[t]he basic reasons for Europe's remarkable military successes are well understood. One was European filth, which caused epidemics that decimated the much healthier populations of the Western hemisphere" (2010: 4).

Then quoting military historian Geoffrey Parker, Chomsky mentions "military superiority" as the second cause, excluding any "social, moral or natural advantage" (ibid.) the European powers might have had in starting the history of violence and in constructing the empire of blood, which we are inheriting today. Although the following statement certainly oversimplifies the complexity of history, it might be said that these are the root causes of the "crisis" that appears today in a singularly new form. In fact, it is not simply the crisis of capital, but rather it is *capital as a historical and human crisis*. This means that the crisis is inherent in the system of capital evident in the fact that the end of production is displaced by the system of capital. Indeed, when you have an increasingly high number of empty houses and homeless people and of wasted food and those who die of starvation, the truth that the aim of production is not consumption but profit can no longer be denied. It is also a sign of the lack of moral authority that defines the European history of domination and conquest all over the world, a sign of the *inhumanity* (Fanon's word; see the following quote) of that history. This has gone beyond Europe, and it has reached global proportions. The Western world (the United States, in particular) has welcomed the seed of that inhumanity and let it grow. As Fanon says in the conclusion to *The Wretched of the Earth*, after noting Europe's failure in the task of inventing a full humanity, "a former European colony took it into its head to catch up with Europe. It has been so successful that the United Stated of America has become a monster where the flaws, sickness, and inhumanity of Europe have reached frightening proportions" (2004: 236–237).

This is the nature of the crisis that has reached frightening and global/imperial proportions. This is not to say that at the outset of the age of conquest and capital things stood differently. As Marx and Engels famously say in *The Communist Manifesto*, addressing the now fashionable theme of globalization, but looking at it from the viewpoint of the inherent violence of its movement, the "need of a constantly expanding market for its products chases the bourgeoisie over the whole surface of the globe. It must nestle everywhere, settle everywhere, establish connections everywhere" (1994: 162). Capital "compels all nations, *on pain of extinction*, to adopt the bourgeois mode of production; it compels them to introduce *what it calls civilization* into their midst, i.e., to become bourgeois themselves" (emphasis added). Marx and Engels add, "In one word, it creates a world after its own image" (ibid.). This is of course something that Fanon often critically addresses in his description and analysis of the colonial and postcolonial world: outside Europe, the European bourgeoisie will only manage to create "a world divided in two" (Fanon 2004: 3). What it calls "civilization," the paradigm of sovereignty, remains constantly linked to the threat of extinction, which often goes from being a threat to its actual and full realization. Indeed, as Benjamin says, civilization is always at the same time barbarism (1968: 256). When the "civilizing" project succeeds, it produces a monster or a caricature (Fanon 2004: 119); in all cases, it produces misery for the vast majority of people. From Fanon's point of view, the truth is that "Europe is literally the creation of the Third World" (58), thus the opposite of what the perverse logic of capital would like to believe. More generally, this means that capital and its wealth are the creation of labor, not simply of productive labor but of life as labor. It is in and through *dispossession*, as David Harvey shows, that wealth is finally concentrated in a few hands—namely, the 1 percent.

Harvey's concept of *accumulation by dispossession*—a renaming of Marx's "primitive" or "original" accumulation (see Marx 1977)—precisely stresses the *ongoing* nature of the accumulation process and thus the ongoing nature of the violence immanent to it. It is precisely because this process continues that Marx's notion of "primitive" or "original" accumulation must be renamed, for those are "peculiar" terms given the context (Harvey 2003: 144).

According to Harvey, "Accumulation by dispossession can occur in a variety of ways and there is much that is both contingent and haphazard about its *modus operandi*" (149). One of the ways in which capitalist accumulation happens (and certainly one of the ways in which it has historically happened) is described by Marx in the first volume of *Capital*. Speaking of the way in which accumulation by dispossession helps with the problem of overaccumulation, Harvey says, "What accumulation by dispossession does is to release a set of assets (including labour power) at very low (and in some instances zero) cost." He goes on to say how, in "the case of primitive accumulation as Marx described it, this entailed taking land, say, enclosing it, and expelling a resident population to create a landless proletariat, and then releasing the land into the privatized mainstream of capital accumulation" (ibid.). It is this ongoing process of enclosure and privatization that is described by the concept of accumulation by dispossession. Harvey then speaks of the collapse of the Soviet Union, the opening up of China, the crisis of overaccumulation since 1973, and the unfinished war in Iraq. In this sense, what Harvey says is close to Naomi Klein's (2008) concept of disaster capitalism, which in turn is already present in Marx and Engels when they say that capitalist crises of overproduction and overaccumulation are overcome "by paving the way for more extensive and more destructive crises" (1994: 164).

Thus if today the struggle for global dominance is singularly new, it is because the constant threat and reality of terror are employed in ever more sophisticated and conscious (and often desperate) ways. War itself is always global, regardless of where it happens. Moreover, in its self-awareness, terror has become, more than it has ever been, a global instrument of racism and xenophobia. Indeed, what is new in the singularity of this violent struggle and this racist and terrifying war is that there is a cleansing of immense proportion going on in the usual attempt to neutralize the enemy (the other); it is a *biopolitical* cleansing—to use a word that has become popular since Foucault. This does not stop at the (in itself) horrifying but "traditional" ethnic cleansing, where one ethnic group is targeted by a state power; rather, each instance of this traditional ethnic cleansing is part of the general paradigm of racist and xenophobic violence. It is part of a global cleansing, where the sovereign elites, the global sovereigns in the political and financial arenas (capital and the political institutions), *in all kinds of ways* target those who do not belong with them on account of their race, class, gender, and above all, on account of their way of life and way of thinking. The reference to the way of life and thinking does not mean to empty racist violence of its true and material substance. In other words, it does not imply an idealist turn. Indeed, the so-called war on terror is a clear example of what targeting people for the way they think and live means (see the chapter on Iraq in Klein 2008). Moreover, the whole history of terror, which is the history of sovereignties, unleashed by the European conquests at the beginning of the modern age (the age of capital) is another tragic proof of the truth that people's ways of life and thinking become the object of racist and genocidal violence for the purpose of accumulation and control. Fanon says, "*It is the racist who creates his inferior*" (1967: 93; emphasis in the original). Thus I am not claiming that specific racism—namely, the systematic use of discrimination and violence against particular ethnic groups on the basis of supremacist ideologies—has given way to a more generic (and thus perhaps weaker) form of racism. Instead, what I am saying is that the paradigm of sovereignty (capital and political power) is inherently racist and inherently violent. Indeed, sovereignty means supremacy, and it is vital for it to exert its control over those it subjugates to the point of annihilation. These are the multitudes of people who, for one reason or the other, are liable for scrutiny and surveillance, extortion (typically, in the form of overtaxation, fines, and debt), arrest, brutality, torture, and violent death. The sovereigns target anyone who, as Agamben (1998) shows with the figure of *Homo Sacer*, can be killed without being sacrificed and be reduced to the paradoxical and ultimately impossible condition of bare life, whose only horizon is death itself. In this sense, the biopolitical cleansing is also immediately a thanatopolitical instrument.

The biopolitical struggle for dominance is a fight to the death. To begin with, those who wage the struggle and those who want to dominate will not rest until they have prevailed. Their fanatical and self-serving drive is also very much the source of the crisis investing all others. The point is to show that the present crisis, which is systemic and permanent and thus something more than a mere crisis, cannot be solved unless the struggle for dominance is eliminated. The elimination of such struggle implies the demise of the global sovereigns (the global elites), and this will not happen without a global revolution, a "restructuring of the world" (Fanon 1967: 82). This must be a revolution *against* the paradigm of violence and terror typical of the global sovereigns. It is not a movement that uses violence and terror but rather one that *counters* the primordial terror and violence of the sovereign elites by living up to the vision of a new world already worked out and cherished by multitudes of people. This is the nature of counterviolence: not to use violence in one's own turn, but to deactivate and destroy its mechanism. At the beginning of the modern era, Niccolò Machiavelli saw the main distinction between dominance and the will to dominate (or the lack thereof) in society.[13] According to Machiavelli, freedom is obviously on the side of those who reject the paradigm of domination. I quote again a passage I have already quoted in Chapter 1: "And doubtless, if we consider the objectives of the nobles [or elite] and of the people, we must see that the first have a great desire to dominate, while the latter have only the wish not to be dominated, and consequently a greater desire to live in the enjoyment of freedom" (1950: 121–122; translation slightly modified).

Who can resist applying this amazing insight to the many situations of resistance and revolt that have been happening in the world for the last few years? From Tahrir Square to Bahrain and from Syntagma Square and Plaza Mayor to the streets of New York and Oakland, "the people" speak with one voice against "the nobles"; the 99 percent all face the same enemy: the same 1 percent; and courage and freedom face the same police and military machine of cowardice and deceit, brutality, and repression. Those who do not want to be dominated, and *do not need* to be governed, are ontologically on the terrain of freedom, always already turned toward a poetic desire for the common good and the ethics of a just world. The point here is not to distinguish between good and evil but to understand the twofold nature of power. This understanding also implies a choice, which is not made in the abstract and vacuum but in the reality of struggle and resistance: the choice between power as domination or as care.

The biopolitical (and thanatopolitical) struggle for dominance is unilateral, for there is only one side that wants to dominate. The other side—ontologically, if not circumstantially, free and certainly wiser—does not want to dominate; rather, it wants *not to be dominated*. This means that it rejects domination as such. The rejection of domination also implies the rejection of violence, and I have already spoken earlier of the meaning of counterviolence in this sense. To put it according to Herman Melville's (2012) Bartleby, this other side "would prefer not to" be dominated, and it "would prefer not to" be forced into the paradigm of violence. Yet for this preference, this desire to pass from potentiality into actuality, action must be taken—an action that is a return and a going under, an uprising and a hurricane. Revolution is to turn oneself away from the terror and violence of the sovereign elites toward the horizon of freedom and care, which is the pre-existing ontological ground of the difference mentioned by Machiavelli between the nobles and the people. What is important is that the sovereign elite and its war machine, its police apparatus, and its false sense of the law are elimi-nated. It is important that the sovereigns be shown, as Agamben says, in "their original proximity to the crimi-nal" (2000: 107) and that they be dealt with accordingly. For this to happen, a true sense of the law must be recu-perated, one whereby the law is also immediately ethics. The sovereigns will be brought to justice. The process is long, but it is in many ways already under way. The recent news that a human rights lawyer will lead a UN investiga-tion into the question of drone strikes and other forms of targeted killing is an indication of the fact that the move-ment of those who do not want to be dominated is not without effect.[14] An initiative such as this is perhaps nec-essarily timid at the outset and it may be sidetracked in many ways by powerful interests in its course. Yet even positing at an institutional level, the possibility that drone strikes are a form of unlawful killing and a war crime is a clear indication of what *common reason* (one is tempted to say, the general intellect) already understands and knows. The hope of those who "would prefer not to" be involved in a violent practice such as this is that those responsible for it be held accountable and that the horizon of terror be canceled and overcome. Indeed, the earth needs care, and when instead of caring for it resources are danger-ously wasted and abused, it is imperative that those who know and understand *should* revolt—and what they must revolt against is the squandering and irresponsible elites and the sovereign discourse, whose authority, beyond all

nice rhetoric, ultimately rests on the threat of military terror and police brutality.

The sovereign everywhere, be it the political or financial
elite, fakes the legitimacy on which its power and authority
supposedly rest. In truth, they rest on violence and terror or the threat thereof. This is an obvious and essential
aspect of the singularity of the present crisis. In this sense,
the singularity of the crisis lies in the fact that the struggle
for dominance is at one and the same time impaired and
made more brutal by the lack of hegemony (i.e., by the
lack of a power able to fully legitimize itself). This is true
in general, but it is perhaps particularly true with respect
to the greatest power on earth, the United States, whose
hegemony has diminished and is progressively vanish-
ing. It is a fortiori true of whatever is called the West, of
which the United States has for about a century been the
vanguard. Lacking hegemony, the sheer drive for domination has to show its true face, its raw violence. The usual,
traditional ideological justifications for dominance (such
as bringing democracy and freedom here and there) have
now become very weak because of the contempt that the
dominant nations (the United States and its most powerful allies) regularly show toward legality, morality, and
humanity. Of course, the so-called rogue states, thriv-
ing on corruption, do not fare any better in this sense.
But for them, when they act autonomously and against
the dictates of the West, the specter of punishment,
in the form of retaliatory war or even indictment from the
International Criminal Court, remains a clear limit, a possibility. Not so for the dominant nations: Who will stop
the United States from striking anywhere at will, Israel
from regularly massacring people in the Gaza Strip and the
occupied West Bank, or envious France from once again
trying its luck in Africa? Yet though still dominant, these
nations are painfully aware of their structural, ontological,
and historical, weakness. All attempts at concealing that

weakness (and the uncomfortable awareness of it) only heighten the brutality in the exertion of what remains of their dominance.[15] Although they rely on a highly sophisticated military machine (the technology of drones is a clear instance of this) and on an equally sophisticated diplomacy, which has traditionally been and increasingly is an outpost for military operations and global policing (now excellently incarnated by AFRICOM), they know that they have lost their hegemony. The loss of hegemony or of the more or less genuine power of persuasion is evinced, for instance, in what the *New York Times* called "a new power in the streets" about ten years ago, as millions of people marched worldwide on February 15, 2003, against Bush's decision to invade Iraq.[16] It is also evident in the new forms of resistance at the level of information and the web incarnated by the awesome power of organizations such as Wikileaks, as well as the possibility (unheard of in the past) of expressions of freedom that are true breakthroughs, such as Bradley Manning's brave leaking of classified documents to Wikileaks and thus the media and the world and Edward Snowden's disclosure of the NSA global system of surveillance. Another important sign of the possible loss of hegemony by the US-led empire can be seen in the rising power of the BRICS (Brazil, Russia, India, China, and South Africa) countries and their own challenge to that empire.

As previously noted, "domination without hegemony" is a phrase that Arrighi uses in his study of the long twentieth century and his lineages of the twenty-first century (2010; 2007). Originating with Ranajit Guha (1992), the phrase captures the singularity of the global crisis, the terminal stage of sovereignty, in Arrighi's "historical investigation of the present and of the future" (2010: 221). It acquires particular meaning in light of Arrighi's notion of the bifurcation of financial and military power. Without getting into the question of the rise of China and East Asia, what I want to point out is that for Arrighi, early in the twenty-first century, and certainly with the ill-advised and catastrophic war against Iraq, "the US *belle époque* came to an end and US world hegemony entered what in all likelihood is its terminal crisis." He continues, "Although the United States remains by far the world's most powerful state, its relationship to the rest of the world is now best described as one of 'domination without hegemony'" (2010: 384).

What can the United States do next? Not much short of brutal dominance. In the last few years, we have seen President Obama praising himself for the killing of Osama bin Laden. While that action was most likely unlawful (Chomsky has often noted that bin Laden was a suspect, not someone charged with or found guilty of a crime), it is certain that one can kill all the bin Ladens of the world without gaining back a bit of hegemony. Obama is less forthcoming about the killing of 16-year-old al-Awlaki, whose fate many have correctly compared to that of 17-year-old Trayvon Martin (killed in Florida by a self-appointed security watchman).[17] But it is precisely in cases like this one that the weakness at the heart of empire, the ill-concealed and uncontrolled fury over the loss of hegemony, becomes visible. Such frenzy denies the possibility of power as care, which is what should replace hegemony, let alone domination. Nor am I sure I share Arrighi's optimistic view about the possible rise of a new hegemonic center of power in East Asia and China; probably that would only be a shift in the axis of uncaring power, unable to affect, let alone exit, the paradigm of sovereignty and violence. Indeed, Arrighi's description and analysis are ultimately limited by what risks remaining a state-centric paradigm: whether it is Genoese, Dutch, British or finally, American or Chinese power, the fact remains that the true source of political and economic power, which is a unity (as well as a pure instance of historical insanity), lies in the violent process of capitalist accumulation. What is needed is a radical alternative in which power as domination, with or without hegemony, is replaced by power as care—in other words, a poetic rather than military and financial shift. A poetic shift is one that recuperates the original meaning of production as *poiesis*, the bringing forth of the useful for the sake of the universal and common good. This is the power whereby that which is made is made with care: the care of the self, who is always social and always equal to another; the other, who is equal to the self; and the world, whose truth is dignity if there is care (and savagery and barbarism in the opposite case—that is, in the case of the capitalist and sovereign paradigm).

Power as care must be based on dignity. But what is dignity? This word must be explained because it is all too easily used, and as such, it might be too vague. Precisely, dignity is the opposite of racism. I use the word *racism* in a very broad sense similar to Benjamin's concept of barbarism—namely, the identity of civilization and barbarism (1968: 256). By it I understand not only the discrimination that takes place on account of a narrow category of race (i.e., of whatever is construed as race) but also all discrimination that happens on account of *difference* when it is falsely understood that there is something—the norm, the same—which by definition is *not* different. The notion of difference, then, immediately acquires a negative connotation. Dignity is the reversal, a countermovement to that. It is the motor of counterviolence. I think it is important to assign dignity an individuating power, and it is in this sense that I prefer to speak of *dignity of individuation* (Gullì 2010). This expression names difference as difference, outside of the decision of the same that turns it into a problematic difference rather than the one that it is. What does this mean concretely? A relevant example comes from Fanon, who says that "[i]n other words, the black man should no longer be confronted by the dilemma, *turn white or disappear*, but he should be able to take cognizance of a possibility of existence" (1967: 100; emphasis in the original).

This is indeed a perfect example of what I mean by dignity of individuation, and it is in the phrase "a possibility of existence" that the notion of power as care is also understood. For what kind of existence is possible for the problematically negative difference that is determined as difference by the gaze and discourse of the same? The answer is no existence whatsoever but rather a tormenting *insistence* in the false activity (thus truly a kind of passivity) of trying to "keep one's place," which is something Fanon does not advise. It is clear that dignity means to stand out. Standing out (and continuing to stand and enduring in it) requires power as well as care. It does not require guns, batons, missiles, and drones. These are the tools of the weak and cowardly and of those who only equivocally belong not only in the human race but also in the truth of existence, its fragility. Thus the standing out of difference, its individuating dignity, is the unsovereign awareness of "a possibility of existence"—unsovereign because enmeshed in the impersonal fragility (yet in the potency) of life itself.

An interesting question is whether it is enough for power not to be sovereign in order to find an exit from all forms of domination. The question is, in other words, that of the relation between sovereignty and domination. It is obvious that there is always domination in sovereignty, and that may come, as we have seen, in a hegemonic or nonhegemonic way. However, can there be unsovereign domination? The answer must be negative, unless one confuses sovereignty with hegemony. Indeed, all forms of violence and domination, even when they happen outside a formalized situation of sovereignty, always carry a residue of the sovereignty paradigm. This is the paradigm of separation, which gives sovereignty its specific meaning, as Jacques Maritain (1998) powerfully shows in *Man and the State.* Thus the power that is grounded in dignity and aims at the destruction of what blocks dignity from fully actualizing itself, insofar as it is nonsovereign, also rejects all violence and domination. Yet the question is perhaps complicated by the distinction found in Foucault between sovereign power and disciplinary power. As far as I can see, this is not a clear-cut distinction, but it is important to deal with it in order to understand a form of power other than the one found in the paradigm of sovereignty and domination and exclusively grounded in dignity and care. Otherwise, one simply goes from sovereign to disciplinary power without perhaps realizing that the two are interlocked. It is true that the power based on dignity and care is similar to the new *nonsovereign* and *nondisciplinary* power sought by Foucault. In *"Society Must Be Defended,"* his 1975–1976 Lectures at the Collège de France, Foucault says that "we should look for a new right that is both antidisciplinary and emancipated from the principle of sovereignty" (1997: 40). As Michael Hardt and Antonio Negri note in *Commonwealth*, one "might suggest to Foucault the Marxist notion of 'counterpower,' but—they continue—that term implies a second power that is homologous to the one it opposes" (2009: 56). As "the other to power," they thus propose "an alternative production of subjectivity," and it is this production that should be understood, according to them, as biopolitics (ibid.). It is, in any case, a power of individuation, the individuating power of care, without which any talk of dignity may simply change nothing. To be sure, Foucault's new and nonsovereign power is not necessarily—certainly not immediately—a counterpower (or antipower) and the power of individuation. In fact, this new power is initially disciplinary power, which at one point (in the eighteenth and nineteenth centuries, Foucault holds) replaces or complements sovereign power (which he sees as a more traditional form of power). Foucault is not very consistent in his views of whether there is a substitution of one form of power with another—disciplinary power taking the place of sovereign power—or whether the two forms coexist, but the latter view seems stronger and indeed applicable even to realities in the twentieth and twenty-first centuries. The shift from one form of power to the other is also a shift from sovereignty to domination and its many forms. Yet as I previously noted, it does not seem to me that they are mutually exclusive. There is always sovereignty in domination. There may be situations in which the classic formula of transcendence and separation, which gives sovereignty its name, is apparently not there. However, in order to try to legitimate sheer domination and raw violence, one always goes back to sovereignty— that is, the right of one subject over another or others (Foucault 1997: 43). Of course, this "one" is mainly and most notably the state and its police machine. Yet the state is not the only one. We find the same situation in the family, the workplace, and other interpersonal relations beyond the family and the workplace, for instance. To be sure, this is all part of the logic of security, state security in particular, and sovereignty. The real effect of this is the opposite of what the logic of power claims. That effect is human insecurity at all levels of everyday life. Hilbourne Watson, for whom "force and violence" are instrumental "in the making of modern statehood organized in capital-ist class societies" (2013: 35), says that "[s]tate security masks violence and domination and provides the necessary cover for the rule of necessity (economic domination and political coercion), subsumes human security under state's security, and covers exploitation and capital accumulation in the tracks of state security" (37). This is part of what today is often referred to as biopolitical power.

Let us see in what sense biopolitical power—a power for which life becomes a problematic object, something to be regulated and controlled in the most efficient and detailed manner—remains inscribed within the formula of sovereign power. Foucault speaks of racism and state racism (1997: 239) in terms of biopolitics as a "new nondisciplinary power . . . applied not to man-as-body but to the living man, to man-as-living-being; . . . to man-as-species" (242). This means to a multiplicity of human beings. Now these human beings are not simply "disciplined, but regularized" (247). It is the power of regularization, the norm, and the power of normalization, although the norm of discipline and the norm of regularization intersect (253). For Foucault, racism is the modality whereby sovereignty survives in the regime of normalization: "If the power of normalization wished to exercise the old sovereign right to kill, it must become racist. And if, conversely, a power of sovereignty, or in other words, a power that has the right of life and death, wishes to work with the instruments, mechanisms, and technology of normalization, it too must become racist" (256).

Basically, "[o]nce the State functions in the biopower mode, racism alone can justify the murderous function of the State" (ibid.). Here Foucault means "also every form of indirect murder" and not "simply murder as such" (ibid.). The following are the instances of indirect murder mentioned by Foucault: "[T]he fact of exposing someone to death, increasing the death for some people, or, quite simply, political death, expulsion, rejection, and so on" (ibid.). It is an interesting list, especially when considered forty years after Foucault wrote it. Indeed, today the racist and murderous modes of the sovereigns—the terror they breathe into everyday and common life—become problems of the most urgent nature. This is indeed what explains the eruption of revolt everywhere in the world in the last few years. In fact, the situation of generalized violence and terror is no longer sustainable. State racism has become common, informing and supporting all instances of institutional violence: war, punishment, the prison, and the police. To say it with Fanon, the world has a racist structure. It is this structure of sovereignty as a generalized mode of domination without hegemony and this gangsterism at the heart of power that must be totally annihilated. The loss of legitimacy of the sovereigns everywhere—including the so-called free and democratic nations—is no longer just a politically interesting phrase but a reality. In addition to police and military brutality, think about the alliance everywhere of governments and the banks, the crippling of everyday life, the imposition of regimes of austerity, the odious debt everywhere, and "the making of the indebted man"—to name the title of a recent and important book by Maurizio Lazzarato (2012). All these things show the wide-ranging scope of sovereign violence and its potentially murderous drive. What is also interesting to note is that the sovereign elites and their guards (the armies and police and bureaucracies everywhere), who are responsible for the global genocidal regimes, are not (per Machiavelli's distinction we have seen earlier) as free as those who "would prefer not to" be dominated and thus find themselves always already within the ontological ground of freedom. Here I would like to quote the words of Aimé Césaire, describing the relation between the European colonists and the enslaved Africans in the age of conquest and slavery: "What sort of men were these, then, who had been torn away from their families, their countries, their religions, with a savagery unparalleled in history? Gentle men, polite, considerate, unquestionably superior to those who tortured them" (Fanon 1967: 130).

The same can be generally said of the relation between the exploiter and the exploited, between the colonizer and the colonized, the torturer and the victim of torture, the warmonger and the victim of war, and so on. The superiority of the latter has to do with a greater and deeper sense of ethics and humanity, the fragility of life, which characterizes those who, precisely, reject domination and thus have a greater desire for freedom.

It is, then, important to ask the question of what power can alter this racism that, as Foucault says, "first develops with colonization, or in other words, with colonizing genocide" (1997: 257). From its first development, we then get to a situation where, as I noted at the outset of this book, racist violence becomes a global and biopolitical regime of terror, a war between two main classes: the war of the political and financial elites against the class of those who have been dispossessed to various degrees— once again, the violence of the 1 percent against the 99 percent. As Foucault says, this is a question of the technique of power more than of ideologies (as it was the case with the traditional type of racism), because the sovereign elites (the state) are well aware of the urgency of the struggle, the fact that, again, what is left to them is the raw use of the violence that, as Benjamin (1978) says, informs the law; in other words, domination without hegemony. Especially at the world's present state, where information and knowledge make it unnecessary and thus impossible for the general intellect or common understanding and reason to be governed, brutal domination and potentially genocidal methods of repression seem to be the only instruments left to a decaying and ruthless global ruling class. Then "the old sovereign power of life and death implies the workings, the introduction and activation, of racism" (Foucault 1997: 258). Foucault gives an example from Nazi Germany, where "murderous power and sovereign power [were] unleashed throughout the entire social body" (259) and "the entire population was exposed to death" (260). But today this is a common and global paradigm: the "sovereign right to kill" (ibid.), from cases of police brutality in the cities to war atrocities throughout the world, has become the most effective way to deal with a "population" that refuses to recognize the false legitimacy of the sovereign, the sovereign right to govern. What Foucault says of the Nazi state—but he acknowledges that it applies to "the workings of all States" (ibid.)—shows the terminal stage of sovereign power: a desperate will to absolute domination no longer able to count on hegemony: "We have an absolutely racist State, an absolutely murderous State, and an absolutely suicidal State" (ibid.). This certainly shows the crisis of sovereignty as state power, but more broadly in a globalized world, it shows the crisis of the sovereign elites. It is a crisis contained within the broader crisis that capitalism itself is. There is no automatic solution to these crises, for there is no self-regulatory modality. Indeed, they will not be solved without the workings of an altering power bound to the desire for freedom and the care of the earth. This is the power of individuation, the dignity of individuation, whose workings are based on resistance and care. It is the power of those who, in the age of biopolitical terror, have "nothing to sell except their own skins" (Marx 1977: 295), reversing the history of racist violence and of "conquest, enslavement, robbery, [and] murder" (ibid.).

Conclusion

Humanity without the Enemy

In this book I reflect on the idea of a politics of human dignity, whose conditions are the overcoming of the enemy thought and the elimination of the split between ethics and politics. The aim of this politics is the making of a world of social justice. This must be a world in which there is no enemy and the enemy thought itself is overcome. Is this a concrete possibility? Even if we start from Carl Schmitt's formulation of politics and the distinction made therein between a political and a personal enemy, the answer would have to be positive. Certainly, even in this different world, it is possible that personal enmities based on passions and interests remain. However, these could be worked out in a number of ways without violence and without war. What is important is to overcome the figure that Schmitt calls the political enemy, which is invariably also an ethical one: the irrecoverably evil one used as an excuse for all kinds of violence and war.

Indeed, another (better) world is possible. The passage to this world of social justice cannot obviously be accomplished in and as a thinking exercise. Contrary to what Schmitt believes, humanity has an enemy, and this enemy will not easily agree to give up its power and disappear. The enemy of humanity is the system of oppression and exploitation, domination and alienation, and humiliation and violence represented today by capital in its neoliberal form. Poverty and debt, the obligation to work in absolutely precarious and alien conditions, enclosure and displacement, homelessness coupled with the lack of free movement, surveillance and control, and so on are all modalities of an existence that looks increasingly inhuman. The ideal of the good life seems increasingly remote and impossible to achieve. Yet the radical inhumanity in which a growing number of people worldwide are forced is also the starting point for a radical change. The fragmentation of actors and subjectivities and interests and desires one finds within this radical inhumanity—a fragmentation also due to the politics of identity, which is yet another configuration of the friend-and-enemy logic—often becomes an impediment to the realization that there is today a class conflict of global proportion. To put it in a perhaps simplistic but telling way, it is the conflict between the 1 percent and the 99 percent. It is still the conflict between capital and labor. What I call humanity in this book is represented by the latter, not the former. It is the living movement, not its reflection and death. Indeed, capital is still the enemy of labor, and the 1 percent is the enemy of the 99 percent. I also often refer to capital and the 1 percent as "the system." Humanity is not this system, but it is what is crushed by it. The system has the means for systemic repression and violence. Like prison, it is violent from beginning to end. It is in fact the exclusive source of systemic and systematic violence. All resistance to it, all counterviolence, by definition is not violent at all; it is something that has nothing to do with violence—except for the fact that it is regularly confronted by the violence of the system itself. In fact, its ontology is radically different, and its history is not—like the history of the law as command—grounded in violence. It is rather grounded in the desire for freedom and the absence of domination—grounded in care, friendship, and love.

Although humanity has an enemy (and that is the system of violent power that crushes it and reduces it to inhumanity), it lacks the structure of the enemy thought. It is perhaps in this sense that Schmitt claims that humanity is not a political concept according to his notion of the political. The structure of the enemy thought understands politics as domination, whose modern specificity lies in the paradigm of sovereignty. However, a nonsovereign way of thinking abandons domination as such in all its forms, but it does not abandon power. Indeed, power and domination are not the same. As Eva Feder Kittay says, "Domination is an illegitimate exercise of power. It is inherently unjust" (1999: 34). Thus it is always an abuse of power. However, nonsovereign resistance retains power as care. Indeed, the movement of resistance is the mode of power capable of overcoming the enemy thought, bringing ethics at the center of politics and politics at the center of ethics. This is the power capable of building a new human community and of turning the world upside down.

Notes

Introduction

1. See Arrigoni (2010).
2. The categorical imperative says, "Act only according to that maxim whereby you can at the same time will that it should become a universal law" (Kant 1981: 30). The principle of the kingdom of ends is, "All rational beings stand under the law that each of them should treat themselves and all others never merely as means but always at the same time as an end in themselves" (39; translation slightly modified).

Chapter 1

1. The reference is obviously to Margaret Thatcher's slogan: "There Is No Alternative" (TINA).
2. See the remark on Machiavelli at the end of this chapter as well as my discussion of some passages by Karl Marx in Chapter 4.
3. See "Machiavelli and the Desire of Freedom" at the end of this chapter.
4. This is Kant's notion, as we will see shortly.
5. See interview in Jamail (2013).
6. In this and the following citations from *The Prince*, I use the word *people* instead of *populace* used by Wootton in his translation.

Chapter 2

1. See Marx (1994a: 38). I will go back to this in Chapter 4.
2. I will give other examples of this utopian way of rethinking and rebuilding communal life in Chapter 5.
3. See Chapter 5.
4. See, for instance, Ryan Gallagher and Glenn Greenwald's recent essay (2014) on the National Security Agency's (NSA) continuing effort to thwart—through a hacking activity that includes posing as a fake Facebook server—people's privacy and freedom

on the Internet, reaching "a new frontier of surveillance operations." Through a variety of malware tools, the agency can "gain total control of an infected computer." Gallagher and Greenwald go on to show the potentially unlimited scale of this type of surveillance, which includes seeking out terror suspects but also people the NSA regards as "extremists," as well as people who do not "pose a threat to national security"—thus, virtually everybody. Moreover, the aim is not always that of surveillance but of disruption.

5. I quote from the text—though a translation—because reading the actual phrasing is, I believe, very important: on the one hand, we have an acknowledgment of the blood ties; on the other, we have the distance created by *the name*.

Chapter 3

1. See, for instance, Associated Press (2005).
2. For an elaboration on the question of losing hegemony, see Chapter 5.
3. See Michel Foucault (1997) and Chapter 5.
4. See, for instance Hsieh (2014).
5. See, for instance, CBS Miami (2011).
6. See Wikipedia, "Death of Kelly Thomas." See also the security camera footage of the beating posted by Voice of OC (2012).
7. Stop and frisk is a practice in New York City that allows police officers to stop and frisk people at any time. Almost all those who have been routinely stopped and frisked in recent years are young African American and Latino men. Consequently, many people see the practice as an instance of racial profiling. Similar practices are obviously present in other US cities and throughout the world.
8. See, for instance, Lucas and Siemaszko (2013).
9. See, for instance, RT (2011).
10. It seems that the new mayor and police commissioner intend to improve the situation by limiting the scope of the stop-and-frisk program in New York City. It is too early to say whether their promise will be maintained. In any case, it is difficult to "improve" a program that is racist and violent at its core and that should simply be abolished. Indeed, there is an irreducible difference between the specificity of a program such as this and the generic character of the law allowing police officers to stop,

question, and search people on the basis of "reasonable suspicion" however problematic the latter still is.

11. See, for instance, Kavanaugh (2012).
12. See, for instance, McKeon (2013).
13. See Devereaux (2013).
14. See González (2012).
15. See Goodman and González (2012a).
16. See Goodman and González (2012b).
17. The best way to get a clear sense of the problem is to watch Jeremy Scahill's movie (also in book format), *Dirty Wars* (2013).
18. See Chapter 5.
19. See, for instance, Serwer (2012).
20. See Becker and Shane (2012).
21. I elaborate on the issue of drone strikes in Chapter 5.
22. Scahill says this toward the end of the movie *Dirty Wars*, as he is reflecting on al-Awlaki's death (*Dirty Wars*: 1: 20: 24–31).
23. For the sake of avoiding any misunderstanding, I am not claiming that there are no criminal terrorist organizations, such as al-Qaeda. However, they are part of the same system I am talking about. They are that system's creatures. They thrive on the system, and the system thrives on them. Together they are a perfect illustration of the pathological functionality of the friend-and-enemy logic.
24. See Goodman and González (2013).
25. See, for instance, Goodman and González (2014a).
26. See Chapter 1.
27. Of course, "staying human" refers to Vittorio Arrigoni's phrase, which I use as an epigraph for the book.
28. In this sense, see the important work by Angela Davis (2003), which proposes an abolitionist approach with respect to the prison system and the logic of punishment as a whole. This approach, she writes,

> would require us to imagine a constellation of alternative strategies and institutions, with the ultimate aim of removing the prison from the social and ideological landscapes of our society. In other words, we would not be looking for prisonlike substitutes for the prison, such as house arrest safeguarded by electronic surveillance bracelets. Rather, positing decarceration as our overarching strategy, we would try to envision a continuum of alternatives to imprisonment: demilitarization of schools, revitalization of education at all levels, a health system that provides free physical and

mental care to all, and a justice system based on reparation and reconciliation rather than retribution and vengeance. (107)

29. Cecily McMillan was then sentenced to three months in jail and five years of probation. See, for instance, Swaine (2014).
30. See Goodman and González (2014d).
31. See Hedges (2014).
32. See Chapter 3, note 22.
33. See, for instance, Edwards (2014).

CHAPTER 4

1. See DPIC (2014).
2. See, for instance, Goodman and González (2014c).
3. In this sense, see the interesting discussion and illustrations in John Holloway's *Crack Capitalism* (2010).
4. See also Stanley Aronowitz (2006).
5. Noam Chomsky often speaks of the Mafia doctrine, or principle, in this sense. See, for instance, Chomsky (2010: 55).
6. In this sense, see the work of Silvia Federici (2004, 2012).
7. See the project of the Basic Income Earth Network in BIEN (2013).
8. See, for instance, Andrea Fumagalli (2013: 102–103) and the contributions of Stefano Lucarelli and Jacopo Mazza, Carlo Vercellone, Andrea Fumagalli, and René Passet in the volume edited by Carlo Vercellone (2006).
9. See Goodman and González (2014b).
10. See, for instance, Goodman and González (2014e).
11. In this sense, see Lazzarato (2012).
12. See Aronowitz and DiFazio (2010).
13. See David and Sapone (2010).
14. See Sasso (2014).
15. See the website for SOS Rosarno: http://www.sosrosarno.org.
16. The 'Ndrangheta is a variety of the Mafia organization, and it is specific to Calabria. Today, it is said to be the most powerful criminal organization in the world.
17. See Wikipedia Contributors, "Gruppi di Acquisto Solidale."
18. Although Hans Lucht's book focuses on Ghanaian fishermen who migrated to Italy and lived in the area around Naples, part two of the book, "The Journey to Europe," is a powerful account of what it takes for African migrants in general to get to Europe. It is divided into two equally powerful chapters: chapter 4,

"The Mediterranean Passage," and chapter 5, "The Maghreb Connection: Libya and a Desert to Cross" (Lucht 2012).

19. This is determined by a European Union Law, the Dublin II Regulation.
20. See Askavusa Collective (2014).
21. For the Italian version of the charter, see Progetto Melting Pot Europa (2014).

Chapter 5

1. See Agamben (2009).
2. See Lazzarato (2006).
3. Ibid.
4. See especially Virno (2004) and Hardt and Negri (2004, 2009).
5. Commenting on the recent *New York Times* article that has revealed the secret "kill list" news, journalist Chris Floyd correctly speaks of "Obama's murder racket" and of a "death squad that Obama is personally directing from the White House." See Floyd (2012).
6. For a discussion of this point, see my chapter on Bataille in Gullì (2010).
7. The phrase is originally from Guha (1992), which is quoted and amplified in Arrighi (2010, 2007).
8. For a discussion, with illustrations, of these forms of abuse of power and impunity, see Chapter 3.
9. See Madhani (2012).
10. See, for instance, Conan (2012).
11. Ibid.
12. See, for instance, the segment on Chile in Klein (2008).
13. See Chapter 1.
14. See Burns (2013).
15. The rise of the Far Right in Europe is yet another example of this weakness and this fear.
16. See Tyler (2003).
17. See Chapter 3.

REFERENCES

Agamben, Giorgio. 1998. *Homo Sacer: Sovereign Power and Bare Life*. Translated by Daniel Heller-Roazen. Stanford, CA: Stanford University Press.

———. 2000. "Sovereign Police." In *Means without Ends: Notes on Politics*. Translated by Vincenzo Binetti and Cesare Casarino. Minneapolis: University of Minnesota Press.

———. 2009. *What Is an Apparatus?*. Translated by David Kishik and Stefan Pedatella. Stanford, CA: Stanford University Press.

Althusser, Louis. 2014. *On the Reproduction of Capitalism: Ideology and Ideological State Apparatuses*. Translated by G. M. Goshgarian. London: Verso.

Aronowitz, Stanley. 2006. *Left Turn: Forging a New Political Future*. Boulder, CO: Paradigm Publishers.

———. 2014. "Where Is the Outrage?" *Situations: Project of the Radical Imagination* 5(2): 19–48.

Aronowitz, Stanley, and William DiFazio. 2010. *The Jobless Future*. 2nd ed. Minneapolis: University of Minnesota Press.

Arrighi, Giovanni. 2007. *Adam Smith in Beijing: Lineages of the Twenty-First Century*. New York: Verso.

———. 2010. *The Long Twentieth Century: Money, Power and the Origins of Our Times*. New York and London: Verso.

Arrigoni, Vittorio. 2010. *Gaza: Stay Human*. Translated by Daniela Filippin. Markfield, UK: Kube Publishing.

Askavusa Collective. 2014. "UNHCR e Frontex al servizio dell'imperialismo." *The Askavusa Blog*, March 19. http://askavusa.wordpress.com/2014/03/19/unhcr-e-frontex-al-servizio-dellimperialismo/.

Associated Press. 2005. "Passengers Recall Tense Moments before Gunfire." *NBC News*, December 8. http://www.nbcnews.com/id/10367598/#.U_5lvDJdVft.

Becker, Jo, and Scott Shane. 2012. "Secret 'Kill List' Proves a Test of Obama's Principles and Will." *New York Times*, May 29.

http://www.nytimes.com/2012/05/29/world/obamas-leader
ship-in-war-on-al-qaeda.html?pagewanted=all.

Benjamin, Walter. 1968. "Theses on the Philosophy of History." In *Illuminations*. Translated by Harry Zohn, 253–364. New York: Schocken Books.

———. 1978. "Critique of Violence." In *Reflections*. Translated by Edmund Jephcott, 277–300. New York: Schocken Books.

Berardi, Franco. 2009. *The Soul at Work: From Alienation to Autonomy*. Translated by Francesca Cadeland Giuseppina Mecchia. Los Angeles: Semiotext(e).

BIEN (Basic Income Earth Network). 2013. Home page. http://www.basicincome.org/bien.

Burns, John F. 2013. "U.N. Panel to Investigate Rise in Drone Strikes." *New York Times*, January 24. http://www.nytimes.com/2013/01/25/world/europe/un-panel-to-investigate-rise-in-drone-strikes.html?_r=1&.

CBS Miami. 2011. "Family Hires Attorney after Police Scuffle with Special Needs Man." September 14. http://miami.cbslocal.com/2011/09/14/family-hires-attorney-after-police-scuffle-with-special-needs-man/.

Chomsky, Noam. 2010. *Hopes and Prospects*. Chicago: Haymarket Books.

Conan, Neal. 2012. "John Brennan Delivers Speech on Drone Ethics." NPR, May 1. http://www.npr.org/2012/05/01/151778804/john-brennan-delivers-speech-on-drone-ethics.

David, Ariel, and Adriana Sapone. 2010. "Immigrants Riot in Rosarno, Italy." *Huffington Post*, March 18. http://www.huffingtonpost.com/2010/01/08/immigrants-riot-in-rosarn_n_416482.html.

Davis, Angela. 2003. *Are Prisons Obsolete?* New York: Seven Stories Press.

Death Penalty Information Center (DPIC). 2014. "Number of Executions by State and Region Since 1976." http://www.deathpenaltyinfo.org/number-executions-state-and-region-1976.

Devereaux, Ryan. 2013. "'We Were Handcuffing Kids for No Reason': Stop-and-Frisk Goes on Trial." *Nation*, March 28. http://www.thenation.com/article/173565/we-were-handcuffing-kids-no-reason-stop-and-frisk-goes-trial.

Duns Scotus, John. 1987. *Philosophical Writings*. Translated by Allan Wolter. Indianapolis: Hackett.

Edwards, David. 2014. "Texas Cop Guns Down 93-Year-Old Woman, but Police 'Not Ready' To Say Whether She Was Armed." *The Raw*

Story, May 7. http://www.rawstory.com/rs/2014/05/07/texas
-cop-guns-down-93-year-old-woman-but-police-not-ready-to-say
-whether-she-was-armed.

Fanon, Frantz. 1967. *Black Skin, White Masks.* Translated by Charles
Lam Markmann. New York: Grove Press.

———. 2004. *The Wretched of the Earth.* Translated by Richard Phil-
cox. New York: Grove Press.

Federici, Silvia. 2004. *Caliban and the Witch: Women, the Body, and
Primitive Accumulation.* New York: Autonomedia.

———. 2012. *Revolution at Point Zero: Housework, Reproduction,
and Feminist Struggle.* Oakland, CA: PM Press.

Floyd, Chris. 2012. "Hymns to the Violence: The NYT's Love Letter to Obama's Murder Racket." *Empire Burlesque*, May 29.
http://www.chris-floyd.com/component/content/article/1
-latest-news/2247-hymns-to-the-violence-the-nyts-love-letter-to
-obamas-murder-racket.html.

Foucault, Michel. 1977. *Discipline and Punish: The Birth of the Prison.*
Translated by Alan Sheridan. New York: Vintage Books.

———. 1997. *"Society Must Be Defended": Lectures at the Collège
de France, 1975–1976.* Translated by David Macey. New York:
Picador.

———. 2004. *The Birth of Biopolitics: Lectures at the Collège de
France, 1978–1979.* Translated by Graham Burchell. New York:
Picador.

Fumagalli, Andrea. 2013. *Lavoro male comune.* Milano: Mondadori.

Gallagher, Ryan, and Glenn Greenwald. 2014. "How the NSA Plans
to Infect 'Millions' of Computers with Malware." *The // Intercept*,
March 12. https://firstlook.org/theintercept/article/2014/03/
12/nsa-plans-infect-millions-computers-malware.

González, Juan. 2012. "Marine Veteran Kenneth Chamberlain Sr.
Killed after Clash with Police Who Responded to His Medical Emergency." *New York Daily News*, April 4. http://www.nydailynews
.com/new-york/marine-veteran-kenneth-chamberlain-sr-killed
-clash-police-responded-medical-emergency-article-1.1055569.

Goodman, Amy, and Juan González. 2012a. "Killed at Home: White
Plains, NY Police Called Out on Medical Alert Shoot Dead Black Veteran, 68." *Democracy Now!*, March 29. http://www.democracynow
.org/2012/3/29/killed_at_home_white_plains_ny.

———. 2012b. "New Details Emerge over Police Fatal Shooting of
Elderly Ex-Marine Kenneth Chamberlain Sr." *Democracy Now!*,
April 6. http://www.democracynow.org/2012/4/6/new_details
_emerge_over_police_fatal.

———. 2013. "'Too Scared To Go Outside': Family of Pakistani Grandmother Killed in U.S. Drone Strike Speaks Out." *Democracy Now!* October 31. http://www.democracynow.org/2013/10/31/too_scared_to_go_outside_family.

———. 2014a. "Turning a Wedding into a Funeral: U.S. Drone Strike in Yemen Killed As Many As 12 Civilians." *Democracy Now!*, February 21. http://www.democracynow.org/2014/2/21/turning_a_wedding_into_a_funeral.

———. 2014b. "Caught in the Crossfire: U.S.-Mexico Border Militarization Threatens Way of Life for Native Tribe." *Democracy Now!*, March 14. http://www.democracynow.org/2014/3/14/caught_in_the_crossfire_us_mexico.

———. 2014c. "Execution Chaos: Witness Recounts Botched Killing that Caused Okla. Prisoner's Fatal Heart Attack." *Democracy Now!*, April 30. http://www.democracynow.org/2014/4/30/execution_chaos_witness_recounts_botched_killing.

———. 2014d. "Occupy Wall Street on Trial: Cecily McMillan Convicted of Assaulting Cop, Faces Up to Seven Years." *Democracy Now!*, May 6. http://www.democracynow.org/2014/5/6/occupy_wall_street_on_trial_cecily.

———. 2014e. "'We Have to Stop This Inequality': Fast Food Worker Strike Spreads to Dozens of Cities." *Democracy Now!*, May 15. http://www.democracynow.org/2014/5/15/we_have_to_stop_this_inequality.

Gordon, Neve, Jacinda Swanson, and Joseph A. Buttigieg. 2000. "Is the Struggle for Human Rights a Struggle for Emancipation?" *Rethinking Marxism* 12 (3): 1–22.

Gramsci, Antonio. 1971. *Selections from the Prison Notebooks*. Translated by Quintin Hoare and Geoffrey Nowell Smith. New York: International Publishers.

Guha, Ranajit. 1992. "Dominance without Hegemony and its Historiography." In *Subaltern Studies IV*, edited by R. Gupta, 210–305. New York: Oxford University Press.

Gullì, Bruno. 2010. *Earthly Plenitudes: A Study on Sovereignty and Labor*. Philadelphia: Temple University Press.

Hardt, Michael, and Antonio Negri. 2004. *Multitude: War and Democracy in the Age of Empire*. New York: Penguin.

———. 2009. *Commonwealth*. Cambridge, MA: Harvard University Press.

Harle, Vilho. 2000. *The Enemy with a Thousand Faces: The Tradition of the Other in Western Political Thought and History*. Westport, CT: Praeger Publisher.

Harvey, David. 2003. *The New Imperialism.* Oxford: Oxford University Press.

Hedges, Chris. 2014. "The Crime of Peaceful Protest." *Truthdig,* April 27. http://www.truthdig.com/report/item/the_crime_of _peaceful_protest_20140427.

Heidegger, Martin. 1977. "Letter on Humanism." In *Basic Writings,* edited by D. F. Krell. New York: Harper and Row.

———. 1996. *Hölderlin's Hymn "The Ister."* Translated by William McNeil and Julia Davis. Bloomington: Indiana University Press.

Hobbes, Thomas. 1994. *Leviathan.* Edited by Edwin Curley. Indianapolis: Hackett Publishing International.

Hölderlin, Friedrich. 1984. *Hymn and Fragments.* Translated by Richard Sieburth. Princeton: Princeton University Press.

Holloway, John. 2010. *Crack Capitalism.* London: Pluto Press.

Hsieh, Steven. 2014. "Albuquerque Police Fatally Shoot Homeless Man Who Was Illegally Camping." *Nation,* March 24. http:// www.thenation.com/blog/178985/albuquerque-police-fatally -shoot-homeless-man-who-was-illegally-camping#.

Jamail, Dahr. 2013. "Ten Years Later, U.S. Has Left Iraq with Mass Displacement & Epidemic of Birth Defects, Cancers." *Democracy Now!,* March 20. http://www.democracynow.org/2013/3/20/ ten_years_later_us_has_left.

Jameson, Fredric. 2010. "A New Reading of Capital." *Mediations* 25 (1): 5–14.

Kant, Immanuel. 1981. *Grounding for the Metaphysics of Morals.* Translated by James W. Ellington. Indianapolis: Hackett.

———. 1996. *Critique of Practical Reason.* Translated by T. K. Abbott. Amherst, NY: Prometheus Books.

Karatani, Kojin. 2005. *Transcritique: On Kant and Marx.* Translated by Sabu Kohso. Cambridge: MIT Press.

Kavanaugh, Shane Dixon. 2012. "NYPD Officers Stop-and-Frisk Harlem Teen, Threaten to Break His Arm: Audio Recording." *New York Daily News,* October 9. http://www.nydailynews.com/ new-york/uptown/cops-stop-and-frisk-harlem-teen-threaten -break-arm-audio-recording-article-1.1178891.

King, Martin Luther, Jr. 1992. "Letter from a Birmingham Jail (1963)." In *I Have a Dream: Writings and Speeches That Changed the World,* edited by James M. Washington. New York: HarperOne.

Kittay, Eva Feder. 1999. *Love's Labor: Essays on Women, Equality, and Dependency.* New York: Routledge.

Klein, Naomi. 2008. *The Shock Doctrine: The Rise of Disaster Capitalism.* New York: Picador.

Lazzarato, Maurizio. 2006. "Biopolitics/Bioecomomics: A Politics of Multiplicity." *Generation Online*, http://www.generation-online .org/p/fplazzarato2.htm.

———. 2012. *The Making of the Indebted Man*. Translated by Joshua David Jordan. Los Angeles: Semiotext(e).

Leibniz, G. W. 1972. *Political Writings*. Edited by Patrick Riley. Cambridge: Cambridge University Press.

———. 1989. "Discourse on Metaphysics." In *Philosophical Essays*. Translated by Roger Ariew and Daniel Garber. Indianapolis: Hackett.

Lucas, Lisa, and Corky Siemaszko. 2013. "Trayvon Martin Shooting: Prosecutors Deride George Zimmerman as 'Wannabe Cop' Who Killed Teen out Buying Skittles during Closing Argument." *New York Daily News*, July 11. http://www.nydailynews.com/ news/national/closings-heard-zimmerman-trial-article-1 .1396074#ixzz3BbLvCz36.

Lucht, Hans. 2012. *Darkness before Daybreak: African Migrants Living on the Margins in Southern Italy Today*. Berkeley: University of California Press.

Machiavelli, Niccolò. 1950. *The Prince and the Discourses*. New York: Random House.

———. 1995. *The Prince*. Translated by David Wootton. Indianapolis: Hackett.

Madhani, Aamer. 2012. "Obama Administration Details Rationale for Covert Drone War." *USA Today*, April 30. http://content.usatoday .com/communities/theoval/post/2012/04/obama-administration -details-rationale-for-covert-drone-war/1#.VABWkvldVft.

Maritain, Jacques. 1998. *Man and the State*. Washington, DC: Catholic University of America.

Marx, Karl. 1973. *Grundrisse: Foundations of the Critique of Political Economy*. Translated by Martin Nicolaus. New York: Vintage Books.

———. 1975. "Critique of Hegel's Doctrine of the State." In *Early Writings*. Translated by Rodney Livingstone and Gregor Benton. New York: Vintage Books.

———. 1977. *Capital, Vol. I*. Translated by Ben Fowkes. New York: Vintage.

———. 1994. "On the Jewish Question." In *Selected Writings*, edited by Lawrence H. Simon. Indianapolis: Hackett.

———. 1994a. "Toward a Critique of Hegel's Philosophy of Right: Introduction." In *Selected Writings*, edited by Lawrence H. Simon. Indianapolis: Hackett.

———. 1994b. "Economic and Philosophical Manuscripts." In *Selected Writings*, edited by Lawrence H. Simon. Indianapolis: Hackett.

Marx, Karl, and Friedrich Engels. 1994. "The Communist Manifesto." In *Selected Writings*, edited by Lawrence H. Simon. Indianapolis: Hackett.

McKeon, Lucy. 2013. "Will There be Justice for NYPD Victim Ramarley Graham?" *Nation*, August 21. http://www.thenation.com/article/175778/will-there-be-justice-nypd-victim-ramarley-graham#.

Melville, Herman. 2012. *Bartleby, the Scrivener: A Story of Wall Street*. New York: Create Space Independent Publishing Platform.

Mumford, Lewis. 1938. *The Culture of Cities*. New York: Harcourt Brace.

Plato. 2002. "Apology." In *Five Dialogues*. Translated by G. M. A. Grube. Indianapolis: Hackett.

Progetto Melting Pot Europa. 2014. "La carta di Lampedusa." Meltingpot.org., February 1. http://www.meltingpot.org/La-Carta-di-Lampedusa-18912.html#.U_-7KzJdVfv.

RT. 2011. "Bloomberg: 'I Have My Own Army'." November 30. http://rt.com/usa/bloomberg-nypd-army-york-599/.

Sasso, Michele. 2014. "Tra topi e abbandono: così si vive nelle bidonville di casa nostra." *L'Espresso*, March 13. http://espresso.repubblica.it/attualita/2014/03/13/news/tra-topi-e-abbandono-cosi-si-vive-nelle-bidonville-di-casa-nostra-1.157055.

Scahill, Jeremy. 2013. *Dirty Wars: The World Is a Battlefield*. New York: Nation Books.

———. 2013. *Dirty Wars*. DVD. Written by Jeremy Scahill and David Riker. Directed by Rick Rowley. Orland Park, Illinois: MPI Home Video.

Schmitt, Carl. 1996. *The Concept of the Political*. Translated by George Schwab. Chicago: University of Chicago Press.

———. 2005. *Political Theology: Four Chapters on the Concept of Sovereignty*. Translated by George Schwab. Chicago: University of Chicago Press.

Serwer, Adam. 2012. "Former Obama White House Spokesman Justifies the Killing of a Teenager." *Mother Jones*, October 25. http://www.motherjones.com/mojo/2012/10/former-obama-spokesman-justifies-killing-teenager.

Sophocles. 2001. *Antigone*. Translated by Paul Woodruff. Indianapolis: Hackett.

Swaine, Jon. 2014. "Occupy Activist Cecily McMillan Sentenced to Three Months in Jail." *The Guardian*, May 19. http://www .theguardian.com/world/2014/may/19/occupy-cecily-mcmillan -sentenced-three-months-prison.

Tyler, Patrick E. 2003. "Threats and Responses: New Analysis; A New Power in the Streets." *New York Times*, February 17. http://www .nytimes.com/2003/02/17/world/threats-and-responses-news -analysis-a-new-power-in-the-streets.html.

Vercellone, Carlo, ed. 2006. *Capitalismo cognitivo: Conoscenza e finanza nell' epoca postfordista*. Rome: Manifestolibri.

Virno, Paolo. 2004. *A Grammar of the Multitude: For an Analysis of Contemporary Forms of Life*. Translated by Isabella Bertoletti, James Cascaito, and Andrea Casson. New York: Semiotext(e).

Voice of OC. "Raw Video; Kelly Thomas Police Beating," YouTube video, 33: 32. May 27, 2012. https://www.youtube.com/watch?v =KU0Imk2Bstg.

Watson, Hilbourne. 2013. "Transnational Capitalist Globalization and the Limits of Sovereignty: State, Security, Order, Violence, and the Caribbean." In *Caribbean Sovereignty, Development and Democracy in an Age of Globalization*, edited by Linden Lewis. New York: Routledge.

Wikipedia. "Death of Kelly Thomas." Accessed 28 August, 2014. http://en.wikipedia.org/wiki/Death_of_Kelly_Thomas.

———. "Gruppi di Acquisto Solidale." http://en.wikipedia.org/ wiki/Gruppi_di_Acquisto_Solidale.

Index

CPSIA information can be obtained at www.ICGtesting.com
Printed in the USA
BVOW08*0153130315

391509BV00005B/29/P